HORSES

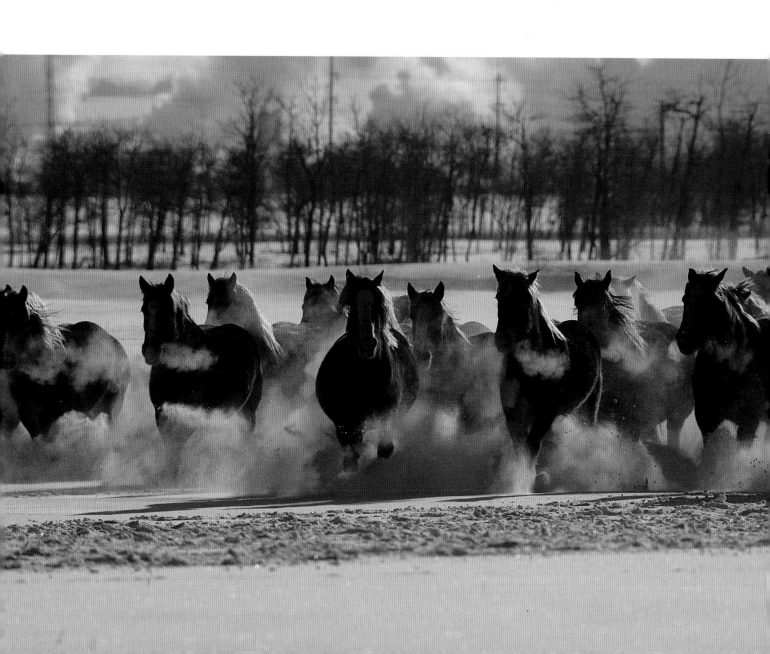

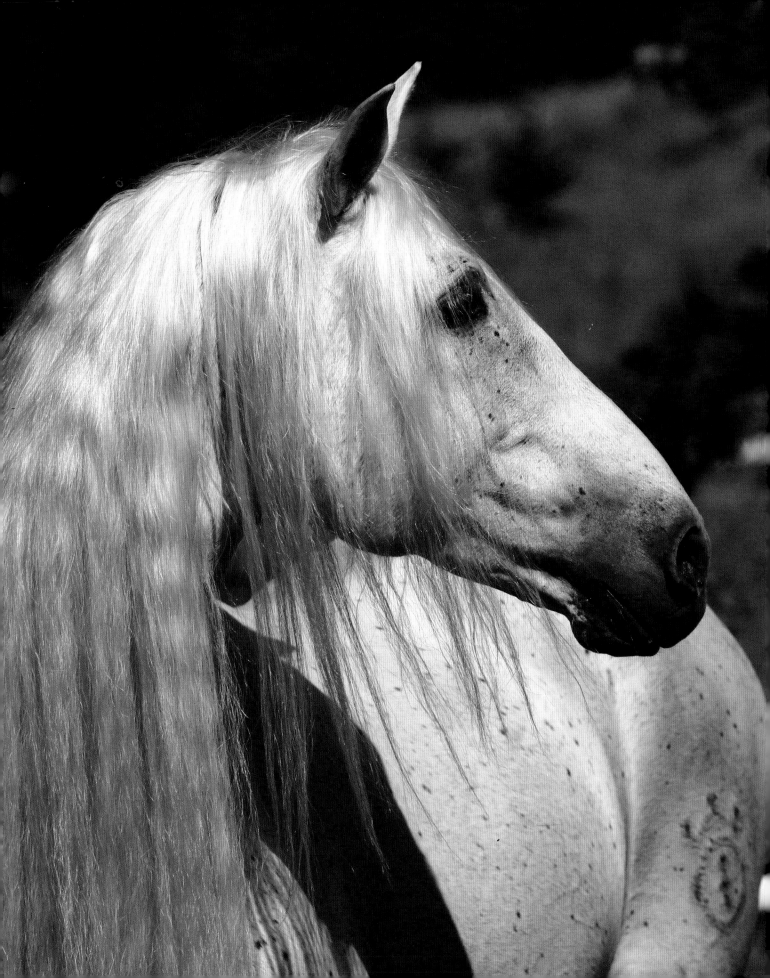

HORSES

BOB LANGRISH   NICOLA JANE SWINNEY

B L O O M S B U R Y

LONDON • NEW DELHI • NEW YORK • SYDNEY

First published in 2014 by Bloomsbury Publishing Plc

50 Bedford Square, London WC1B 3DP

www.bloomsbury.com

Copyright © 2014 in text: Nicola Jane Swinney
Copyright © 2014 in photographs: Bob Langrish
Copyright © 2014 Bloomsbury Publishing Plc

Bloomsbury is a trademark of Bloomsbury Publishing Plc

Bloomsbury Publishing, London, New Delhi, New York and Sydney

A CIP catalogue record for this book is available from the British Library

ISBN 978-1-4729-0984-8

Printed in China by Toppan Leefung Printing Co Ltd.

This book is produced using paper that is made from wood grown in managed sustainable forests. It is natural, renewable and recyclable. The logging and manufacturing processes conform to the environmental regulation of the country of origin.

10 9 8 7 6 5 4 3 2 1

PRELIMINARY PAGE IMAGES

Page 1: Belgian; page 2: Andalusian;
page 5, top: Tennessee Walking Horse;
page 5, below: Chincoteague.

Note on measurements

Imperial measurements are traditionally used in the equestrian world, with races, for example, always being expressed in miles, yards and furlongs. Horses are traditionally measured as 'hands high' (hh) at the shoulder, with a hand being 4 inches.

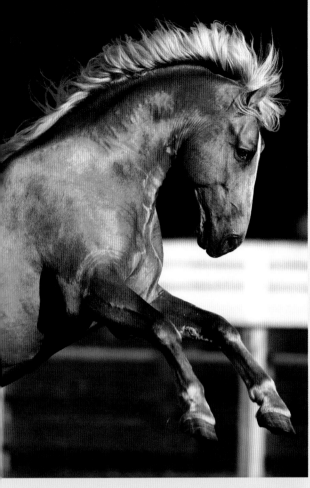

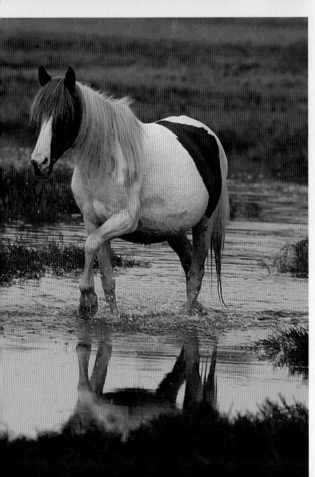

Contents

Introduction

In his iconic poem *In Praise of the Horse*, Ronald Duncan says about the horse that 'All our history is his industry'. The phrase perfectly sums up our eternal relationship with equines; throughout human history, worldwide, the horse has been there with us – at work, at war and at leisure. While the dog is universally known as 'man's best friend', perhaps the horse better deserves this epithet. This book profiles more than 70 of the world's horse breeds, describing their history, development, characteristics and relationship with humans.

THE EVOLUTION OF THE HORSE

It is now widely accepted that the first ancestor of today's horse, *Equus*, was *Hyracotherium*, also known as *Eohippus*, or 'Dawn Horse'. Dating back to the Eocene epoch 56–34 million years ago, this creature bore little resemblance to the modern equine. Living in the forests of North America, it was somewhat doglike, with a short neck, arched back, short legs and long tail. It had four toes on each front foot and three behind, and walked on 'pads' like a dog.

Hyracotherium was a grazer living on fruits and soft foliage, and was a successful forest dweller, changing little for around 20 million years. Then the climate of North America changed, becoming drier. The vast tracts of forest shrank and grasses evolved. *Hyracotherium* grew taller and leggier so that it could run faster in the open, where it was at its most vulnerable, and its teeth became tougher to enable it to grind down grasses. At this stage it became known as *Mesohippus*.

It should be noted that the evolution from *Hyracothium* to the modern *Equus* is not a progression along a neat straight line, even though it is often depicted as such. Rather, *Equus* is but a branch of the evolutionary tree. For example, after *Mesohippus* came *Miohippus*, a change that occurred quite suddenly in evolutionary terms. *Miohippus* was larger than its older cousin, with a longer skull, its ankle joints altered and its teeth changed. Fossil evidence shows that these two animals overlapped, rather than *Mesohippus* gradually morphing into *Miohippus*.

Later transformations saw the horse begin to walk on 'tiptoe', using its middle toe rather than its pads to enable it to run fast; its leg bones fused and its musculature strengthened to make it a swift runner. Around 17 million years ago came *Merychippus* – the 'horse with a new look'. Standing at around 10hh (or 40 inches high) and as such being the tallest equid yet, *Merychippus* was the first animal to closely resemble the modern *Equus*.

Merychippus underwent rapid transformation and is thought to have developed up to 19 different strains, separated into three groups: three-toed grazers known as 'hipparions', a line of small horses known as 'protohippines' and a line of 'true equines'. This last was a large horse-type species with small side toes, and it gave rise to at least two separate groups. Both groups lost their side toes and developed side ligaments around the fetlock that helped to stabilize the central toe, enabling them to move at speed.

The one-toed horses included *Pliohippus*, which until recently was thought to be a direct ancestor of *Equus*. However, differences in its skull formation and its teeth prove otherwise, although they were obviously related. The second group is *Astrohippus*, which is considered to be a descendant of *Pliohippus*. There is a third, recently discovered strain called *Dinohippus*, around 12 million years old, which bore a compelling resemblance to *Equus*, although its exact ancestor is unknown. *Dinohippus* was the most common strain in North America.

Ten million years ago there was an explosion of diversity within the horse family, both in types and in numbers, which has never since been equalled. Our horse, of the genus *Equus*, developed around four million years ago, and the three-toed 'hipparion' died out altogether. Until about a million years ago, there were *Equus* horses in vast migrating herds all over Africa, Asia, Europe, and North and South America, but as the Ice Age began the horses of the Americas died out, although the cause of this extinction is unknown.

MODERN HORSES

The modern horse, a subspecies of the genus *Equus* (*Equus ferus caballus*) and a member of the family Equidae, is a perissodactyl – a hoofed mammal that bears its weight on its middle toe. Other perissodactyls are the tapir and rhinoceros.

Although there are no longer the numbers or the enormous herds of wild horses that there once were, the sheer diversity of type and breed is astonishing. Przewalski's Horse (page 34) is an *Equus* subspecies (*E. f. przewalskii*). It is our one remaining link to the primitive equines that roamed the vast tracts of Asia, yet its origins remain a mystery. It is almost as far from the beautiful Arab as two members of the same genus can possibly be. The huge Forest Horse of Europe, also known as the Diluvial Horse, is no more. However, its echo can be seen in the mighty

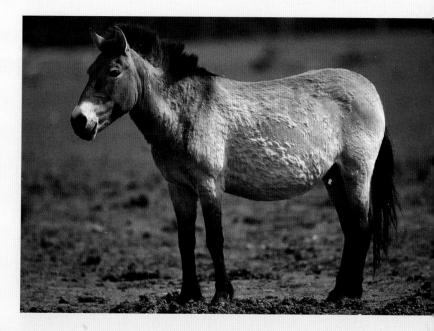

Shire, the world's biggest equine breed. The tiny Shetland of Scotland and the sturdy Exmoor, Britain's feral pony, portray the primitive traits of the ancient *Equus*, while the Americas, which lost their indigenous horses thousands of years ago, now have an equine cornucopia.

It would be wrong to think that the horse is no longer evolving. Witness the meteoric rise of the warmbloods – horses originally bred in central Europe for cavalry purposes by crossing native draught or carriage horses (in equine terminology known as coldbloods), with Arabs or similar breeds (known as hotbloods). Humans certainly played a part in the development of these horses as they bent their talents to their needs. They should be credited for saving many of our most beautiful breeds, such as the Trakehner and Lipizzaner of Europe, as well as

Above Przewalski's Horse, discovered in the 19th century, is our closest link with primitive equines. It has the so-called 'primitive' features of black points, upright mane and dorsal stripe down its back.

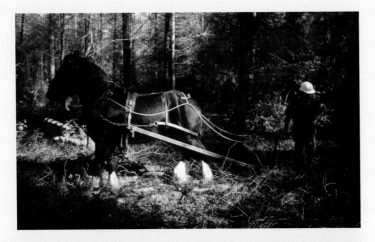

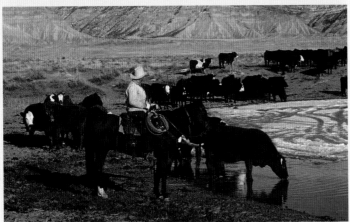

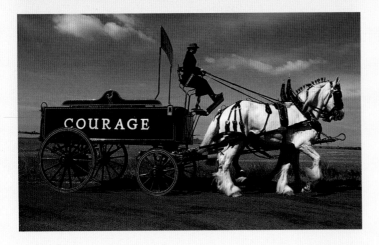

with trying to recreate lost and forgotten horses like the Tarpan (*E. f. ferus*).

THE HORSE IN WORK

When humans decided to harness the horse's power rather than to eat its meat, it was the beginning of an enduring affinity between human and animal that still serves us today. The horse has been our beast of burden, our transport and our warrior.

Ploughing

The many heavy or draught breeds were initially developed for war; they had to carry a knight in full armour into battle, so had to be strong. This strength also proved invaluable when pulling the farmer's plough through soil. The Egyptians are credited with developing the early plough and the Romans brought it to Britain. Ploughing was hard, back-breaking work, and one or two horses took the burden off the farmer. Some breeds of heavy horse, such as the Suffolk, adapted to fulfil their role very efficiently. Now, of course, there are easier ways to prepare soil and the plough horse is largely redundant, although ploughing matches are still held all over the world.

Logging

Far from being an outdated and outmoded relic of a long-forgotten age, horse logging remains a vibrant and continual tradition in the 21st century, with the horse still being used in inaccessible places where the tractor and heavy equipment cannot go. Logging is often carried out in unstable, wet or steep places, and the horse's strength and surefootedness is far

Top left The horse is still used in logging today in places that machinery cannot easily access or where it would cause damage. **Centre left** Ranch hands take a breather – their agile horses are said to possess 'cow sense'. **Bottom left** The dray horse was used by breweries to carry ale.

superior to any vehicle. As well as removing fallen trees, logging can thin out and clear woodland where needed, and extract unwanted, old or diseased timber without damaging sensitive sites. It is far more environmentally friendly than using machinery and is low impact. Horse loggers can perform other forestry services, too, like scarifying soil to encourage natural regeneration, and moving materials.

Dray horses

In London, south of the River Thames, stands a magnificent statue of Jacob, a dray horse. The lifesize statue, which was transported to its new home by helicopter in 1987, marks the site of the old Courage brewery. Like all beer makers of the day, it used dray horses to transport its ales to London pubs. From the Courage stables at Queens Hill in the area of London known as Horseleydown – derived from Horse-Lie-Down – the drays would cross the river at London Bridge into the City. Few breweries now keep the mighty dray horses – often Shires or Clydesdales – and those that do generally use them mainly for publicity purposes.

It was not just beer that dray horses carried. In France the magnificent Boulonnais horse would pull carts of fish from Boulogne to Paris on a trip that became known as the *route de poissons*. The journey from sea to city, a distance of almost 200 miles, had to be made as quickly as possible so that the fish remained fresh. The Boulonnais could complete the trip in 18 hours.

Police work

Whether in central London, New York City or Canada, the horse is an important part of policing worldwide. The oldest recorded mounted unit is the London Bow Street Horse Patrol, established in 1758. Even with mechanization in the 19th century, the horse has never been fully replaced by vehicles. It is used not only for ceremonial duties, but also for crowd control and search and rescue. One of its great strengths in this regard is that it will do everything it can to avoid stepping on a person.

Hunting

Humans have always hunted mammals for their meat and hides, but hunting as a recreational pastime is a relatively new sport. The Tudor kings hunted deer in Britain – the poor were only permitted to hunt rabbit or hare – but it was not until the 17th century that the main quarry species became the Red Fox. An Englishman named Rupert Brooke took modern foxhunting to America in 1650, bringing a pack of hounds and horses to Maryland. Today foxhunting is banned in England and Wales.

Horses in war

Almost from the first time humans went to war, the horse went with them. The earliest evidence of horses being used in war dates from 4000–3000BC in what was Eurasia. The Greek philosopher and soldier Xenophon, of the 4th century BC, is widely credited with the principles of modern horsemanship (page 11), and the efficacy of the horse in war was revolutionized by the invention of modern tack. The world's magnificent heavy horse breeds were originally developed as warhorses, to carry armoured knights, while the Arab, with its speed and stamina, was prized by the Bedouin people for raiding other tribes. In turn, these spirited equines were brought

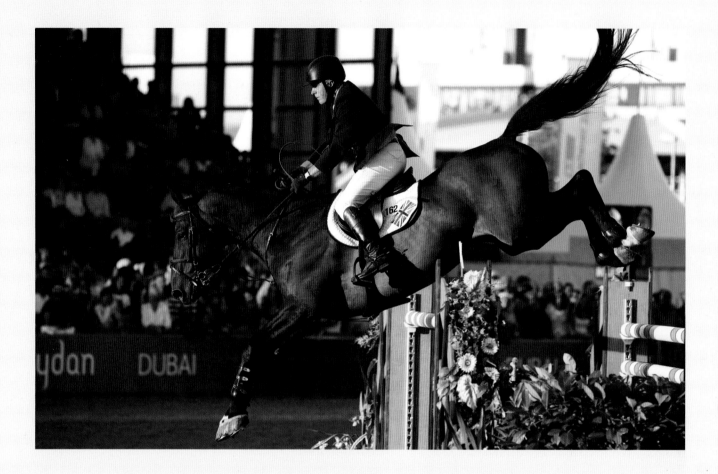

to Britain from the Crusades and formed the base for the world's most revered breed, the Thoroughbred.

Millions of horses perished in the gruelling trench warfare of the First World War, drowning in the mud of France and the Western Front. One of the most successful theatre productions of the 21st century, both in Britain and the United States, is *War Horse*, which is based on a simple story of a boy who goes to war to find and bring back his beloved horse Joey. To quote Ronald Duncan's much-loved poem *In Praise of the Horse*, 'He serves with servility, he has fought without enmity'.

THE HORSE IN SPORTS

Horses are used in competitive sports that developed from their uses in work. These take advantage of the horse's natural abilities: its instincts, speed, stamina and movements in the wild.

Eventing

Military strategists invented the sport we now know as three-day eventing, once called *militaire*. The three phases – dressage, cross-country and

Above The sport of showjumping is quite new – the first competitive class was held at London's Olympia in 1907. Showjumping was first included at an Olympic Games in Stockholm in 1912.

showjumping – were devised to test a horse's obedience, endurance and power. Cavalry horses were required to travel long distances at some pace, often negotiating obstacles in their path, and to be equally able to perform strict parade movements. These are echoed in the dressage test, in which the horse must follow a set plan that shows its flexibility and training. The cross-country course proves the animal's stamina and courage, as well as its ability to tackle obstacles, including water, to show that it can cross the country at speed. In the showjumping phase, the horse must come back on to the bridle and jump accurately and cleanly.

The very highest level of eventing is the CCI four-star, with only six such competitions in the world – Badminton and Burghley in Britain, Rolex Kentucky in the United States, Adelaide in Australia, Luhmühlen in Germany and Pau in France. They are the ultimate test of horse and rider.

Showjumping

Most of the competitors in early showjumping classes were military, and the sport itself is comparatively new. It was not until the English Enclosure Act of 1750 that the incredible athletic agility of the horse was truly recognized. Before this riders did not have to negotiate obstacles to cross the country quickly, but as land became enclosed they had to jump to take the shortest route.

The first showjumping class was held at Olympia in London in 1907; later competitions were divided into military and civilian sections. The very first showjumping contest at an Olympic Games was in 1912 in Stockholm. Today showjumping is one of the most popular equestrian sports.

Dressage

The Greek Xenophon wrote a treatise in about 350BC entitled *On Horsemanship*. It is one of the oldest surviving Western works detailing the principles of classical dressage, including training the horse in a manner that is non-abusive, using kindness and reward. Classical dressage was developed as training for the warhorse – using its impulsion and athleticism as well as its speed and courage. The gymnastic manoeuvres involved – which can be seen today in the Spanish Riding School of Vienna and France's Cadre Noir – were to enable the rider to fight or escape if surrounded.

As a 'fight or flight' animal, the horse holds itself in natural collection, harnessing the power in its hindquarters, the biggest muscles in its body, to make it ready for anything. To impress a mare a stallion pumps up his chest, raises his neck and flexes his poll – the 'collection' seen in a dressage arena. At the same time, the extended trot and canter are natural exaggerations of the gaits. When fighting a horse collects himself to produce lightning fast reactions for kicking, rearing, spinning, striking out with his forefeet, bucking and jumping. This natural agility while playing, fighting and courting can be seen in the dressage arena.

Polo

While the modern game is a favourite of British royals, polo is an ancient sport – the first recorded game was played in 600BC between the Turkmens and the Persians. Polo is thought to have originated in China and Persia, and the word 'polo' derives from the Tibetan word *pholo*, meaning ball or ball game. By the 16th century it had spread to India, and British tea planters discovered it in Manipur, on the India-Burmese border, in the 1850s. The world's oldest polo club is the Calcutta Club, founded in 1862. The game became a great favourite with British soldiers and naval officers based in India, and John Watson of the 13th Hussars drew up the first real rules of polo in the 1870s. Polo was an Olympic sport in 1900–1939; efforts have since been made to reinstate it, though so far unsuccessfully.

Driving

While humans have driven horses to a variety of carts and carriages for centuries, the sport of horse-driving trials, in which horses and ponies are driven to perform a dressage test, an obstacle phase around cones and a gruelling marathon, is relatively modern. Its unique selling point is that anyone aged 14 to 70 years plus, male or female, can compete. The obstacles encountered on the cross-country phase, known as hazards, can include gates, fences, water splashes or a combination. There is a set time in which competitors have to finish the course, and penalties are added for various faults. Driving trials have been under the regulations of the International Equestrian Federation since 1970.

Racing

It is called the 'sport of kings' and it was England's King James I (r. 1567–1625) who is credited with building the first racecourse for the modern sport, changing the fortunes of Newmarket, a small English town. Due to royal patronage, the sport of horseracing became universally popular, as did the breeding of Thoroughbred horses following the importation of Arab stallions that were crossed

with British mares (page 19). Horseracing became the first regulated sport in England when the Jockey Club was formed in the 18th century. The great Classic races – the St Leger, the Oaks and the Derby – were founded in 1776–80.

The first Thoroughbred exported to North America was Bulle Rock, imported by Samuel Gist of Virginia in 1730, and more followed. The United States built her first racecourse in Saratoga, and the first Thoroughbred race was staged in 1847.

Reining

As American as the cowboy himself, reining has its roots in the United States' great ranching history. It is all about the agility and skill of both horse and rider – of being able to turn on a sixpence and stop on a dime – and dates back to the days when ranchers managed herds of cattle on horseback. Cattle were run on the open range, and had to be moved, branded and herded, with the ranchers sometimes having to separate, or cut, one or two from the herd for veterinary attention.

The ranchers' horses needed to be nimble, quick and able to change direction swiftly and occasionally sprint after an errant cow. The cowboys rode one-handed: they had to rope the cattle, so they controlled their horses with their legs and with one hand on the reins. They would have competitions with other ranch hands to prove who was the best and had the fastest horse – this was the birth of the sport of reining.

Reining movements are usually taken at a lope – a slow, collected canter – or a gallop. They include

Right Polo is an ancient game, the first match being recorded in 600BC, but its first set of rules was drawn up by an Englishman in the 1870s. Today, polo is played all over the world and is one of the most exciting sports to watch.

circling, both large and small; sliding stops, where the horse comes to a halt from a gallop, and flying changes, in which the horse switches its leading front and hind legs in mid-stride. The sport can be viewed as a ballet at the gallop.

Endurance

Travelling long distances on horseback was once a necessity – horses were the only form of transport and almost everyone, from the farmer and postman to the doctor, would ride. As riding became a leisure activity, the endurance side of it became one of the fastest growing equestrian sports.

Organized endurance riding as a formal sport began in the 1950s, when the American Wendell Robie and a group of equestrians rode from Lake Tahoe across the Sierra Nevada Range to Auburn in less than 24 hours. Rides vary between 50 and 100 miles and test the fitness of the horse, the judgement of the rider and the performance of both across the country. They are stopped periodically on the course at 'vet gates', where the horse is monitored and has its heart rate measured. If the veterinary surgeons in attendance feel it is detrimental to the horse's health for it to continue, it is not allowed to finish the ride. Any horse can compete in endurance riding, but the Arab, with its speed and stamina, reigns supreme.

What will the future bring for the horse? Those who love horses will wait and wonder.

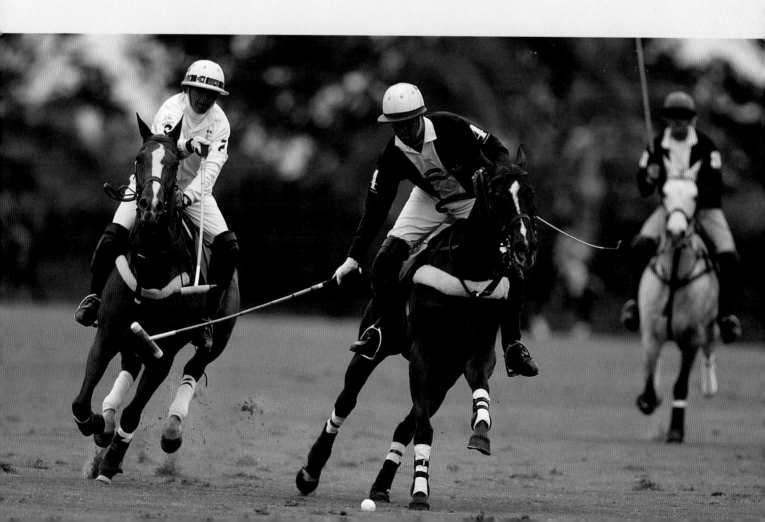

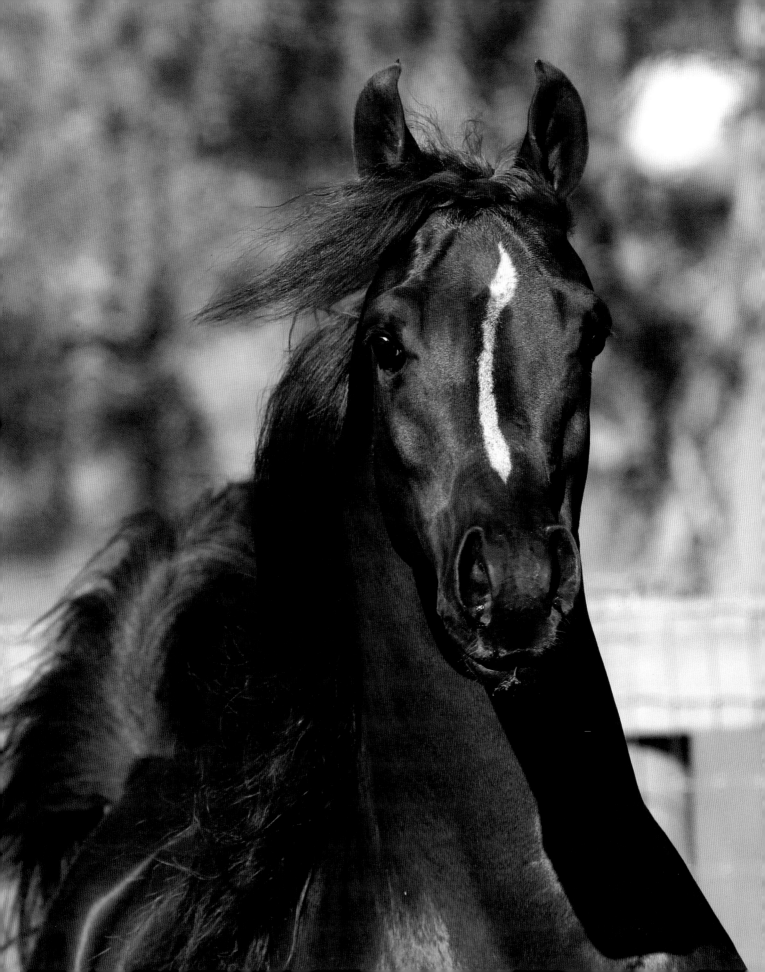

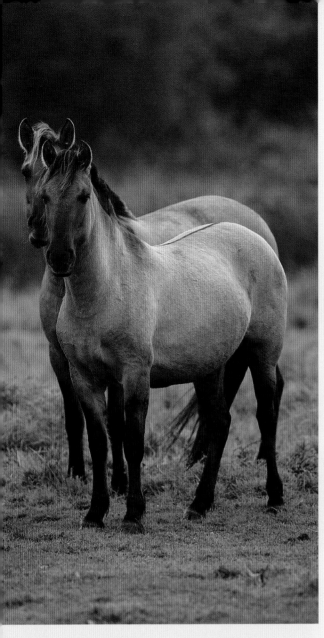

Beginnings

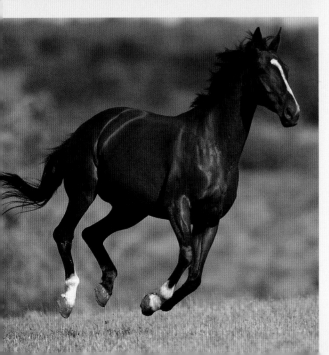

The Arab is one of the world's most beautiful equines and is widely accepted to be the fountainhead of the majority of today's breeds, including the noble Thoroughbred. This desert horse is hotblooded, like the Barb, with which it shares many traits, and the Akhal-Teke.

Clockwise from far left Arab (page 16); Konik (page 31); Thoroughbred (page 19).

Arab

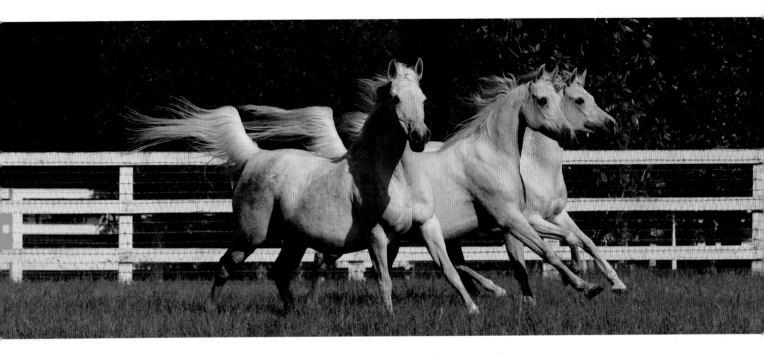

To the Bedouin people of the Middle Eastern desert, the Arab horse was considered a gift from their god; it was almost worshipped, and slept inside the tents with its masters. It retains an affinity with humans today. In the lush oases situated along the Rivers Euphrates and Tigris, which run through the countries now known as Iran, Iraq and Syria, and in the Arabian peninsula, the Arab has become everything desirable in an equine breed.

The Arab was a valued member of a Bedouin family, and the Bedouins kept the breed *asil*, or pure. The tribesmen used horses to raid other tribes, stealing their horses and stock and thus adding to the wealth of their own tribe. They needed their horses to be biddable, but fleet of foot and with great stamina. Mares and not stallions were generally used in raids, because they were less likely to neigh to other horses, giving away their position. They were held in high esteem and valued beyond price. Stock changed hands and each tribe had its own valued line of pure horses. Centuries of selective breeding produced this equine blueprint, a horse of great beauty and speed, whose endurance and strength are matched by its spirit and intelligence.

Above The Arab stands at only around 15hh, but has great presence. Its high tail-carriage is one of its most attractive characteristics, giving it a sense of joie de vivre.

Opposite top The Arab's elegant 'dished', or concave, profile can already be seen in these beautiful foals.

Opposite below Large eyes, a broad forehead and a muzzle that can fit in a teacup make this lovely grey a true representative of the Arab breed.

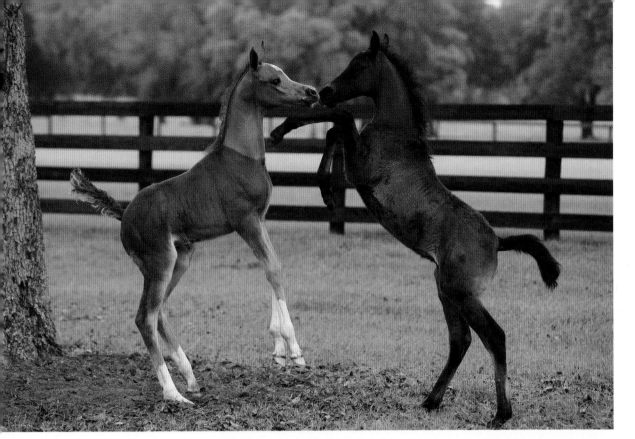

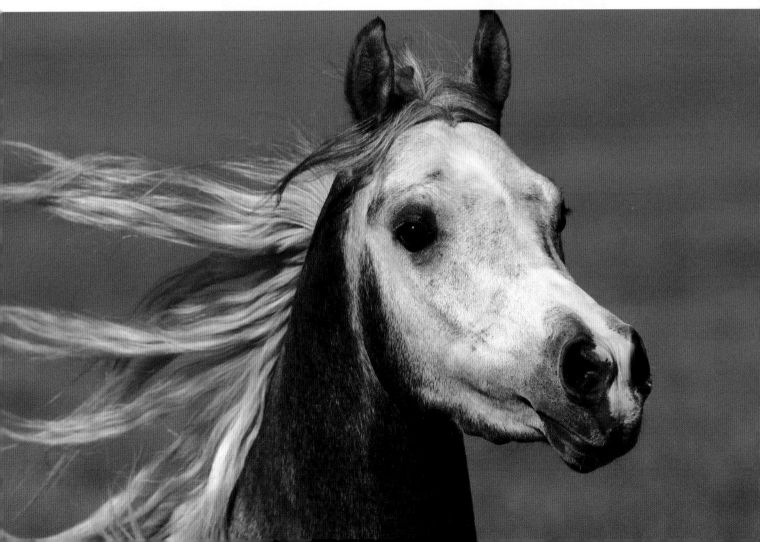

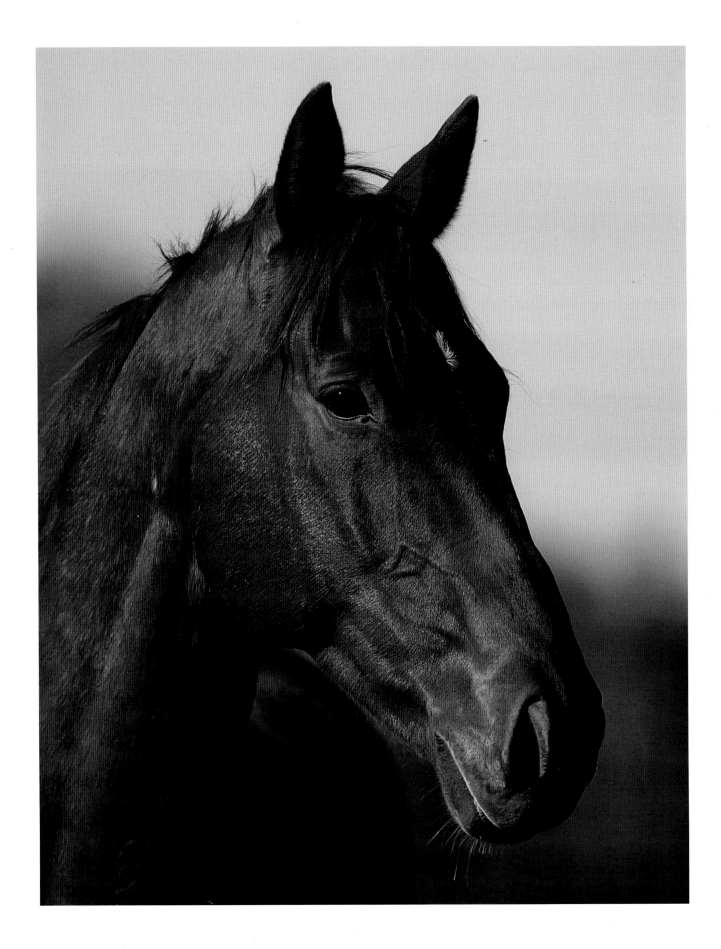

Thoroughbred

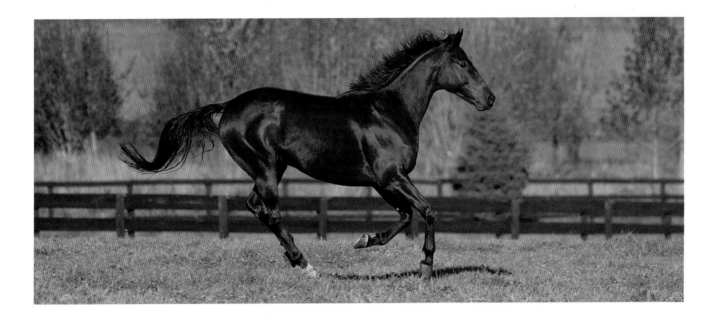

Without the Arab the celebrated English Thoroughbred – on whom a worldwide multi-billion dollar industry is based – would not exist. This equine colossus, whose 'hot' blood has been used to create the mighty warmblood, so desired in equestrian competitions, had its origins in just three stallions – the Darley Arabian, Godolphin Arabian and Byerly Turk. According to the custom of the 17th–18th centuries, these three horses were named after their owners, Thomas Darley, Lord Godolphin and Captain Robert Byerly, and were brought to Britain from the Middle East.

The Darley Arabian was acquired in the Levant (now Syria) in 1704, by the British consul Thomas Darley. The horse was the great-great-grandsire of Eclipse, arguably the most famous racehorse ever. The Godolphin Arabian was sometimes referred to as the Godolphin Barb due to the fact that he was imported from North Africa, but early 18th-century descriptions indicate that he was most likely an Arab. The Byerly Turk, thought by some to be an Akhal-Teke, founded the line from which the first-ever Derby winner, Diomed in 1780, was descended.

These three stallions were the foundation sires on which the Thoroughbred was based. Crossed with the larger British native stock, they produced an equine of considerable beauty that was able to gallop for some distance at great speed.

Opposite The Arab influence is apparent in the Thoroughbred's fine-boned head, neat ears and thin skin.

Above The breed gets its endurance and speed from its Arab ancestors, but it stands taller at 16hh or more and is more strongly muscled, particularly in its hindquarters.

Anglo Arab

Taller than the Arab and also stronger than the Thoroughbred, the Anglo Arab combines the best of both breeds. The breed was founded with two stallions, the Arabs Massoud and Aslam, thought to be Turkish, imported to France from Syria. They were put to three imported English Thoroughbred mares, Comus Mare, Daer and Selim Mare. Their three daughters, Clovis, Danae and Delphine, were to form the foundation stock of the breeding programme at the Pompadour National Anglo Arab Stud, part of the French National Stud.

Louis Gayot, who was appointed manager of Pompadour in 1848, wrote of the Anglo Arab: 'It has a longer figure, high tail carriage, deep and roomy body and bigger legs than the Arab; they are less flat, less out-stretched and less thin than the English Thoroughbreds. They are less touchy and their foals are less irritable.' Gayot is credited with developing the modern Anglo Arab by crossing the progeny of a Thoroughbred-Arab cross back to a Thoroughbred, then crossing the offspring of that mating back to an Arab.

The breed certainly found favour. While it lacked some of the fire of its Arab ancestor, it had its intelligence and trainability, and was found to excel at most equestrian disciplines, including showjumping and eventing. The modern Anglo Arab must be between 25 and 75 per cent Arab.

Right The robust good looks of the Anglo Arab show its exotic heritage, but it stands taller than the Arab at around 16.2hh.

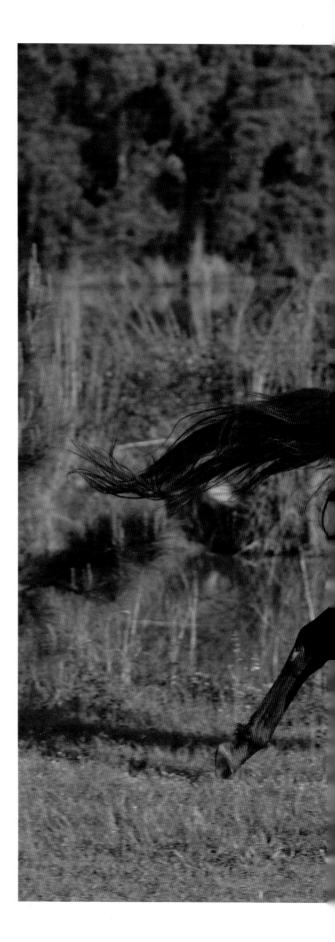

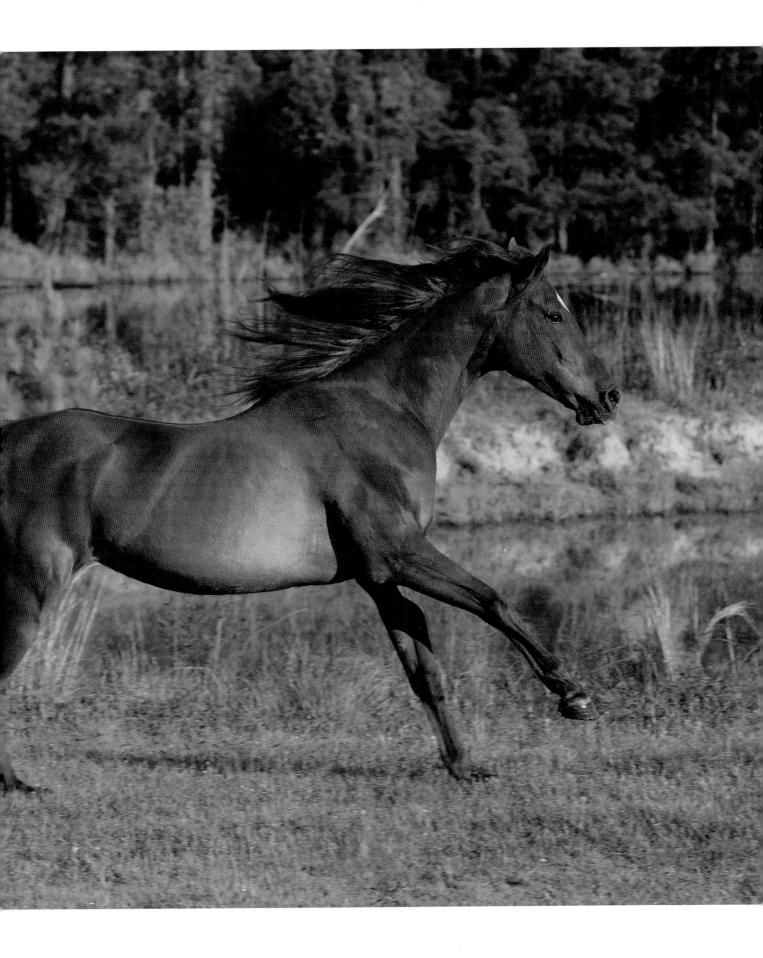

Barb

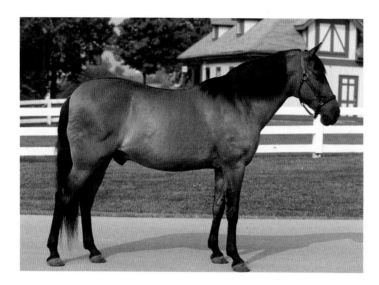

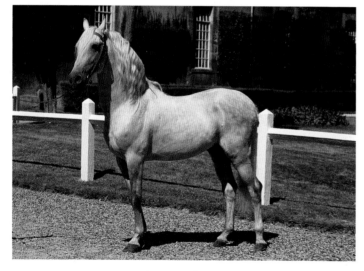

An argument as to whether the Barb breed has a common ancestor with the Arab has never really been satisfactorily settled. It certainly originated in the Maghreb region of North Africa, which borders the Mediterranean Sea and essentially embraces the Atlas Mountains and coastal plain of Morocco, Algeria, Tunisia and Libya. It is a hotblooded desert breed like the Arab, but there the similarity between them ends.

The Barb stands taller than its Middle Eastern cousin and has a convex profile rather than a dished one. It has a longer back and a sloping croup, and does not have the characteristically high tail carriage of the Arab. The confusion between the breeds may have arisen because the North African handlers of the Barb horses spoke Arabic – a number of documents refer to one of the founding sires of the Thoroughbred as the Godolphin Barb, but received wisdom is that he was an Arab, though he originated in North Africa. Nonetheless, it is likely that the Barb, which is renowned for its great speed, hardiness and stamina, has had some influence on the Thoroughbred, as well as on many other breeds.

Experts maintain that the only pure Barbs left are to be found in Cameroon, but the Barb is also bred in Algeria, Morocco, Tunisia and Libya, all of which name the breed their own.

Top The Arab and Barb are similar in that they are both desert-type breeds, but the Barb shows different traits from the Arab.

Above The handsome Barb has undoubtedly been influenced by Arab blood but it is taller, standing at around 15.2–16hh.

Opposite The Barb's head profile is straighter than that of the Arab, as can be seen in the noble stallion shown here.

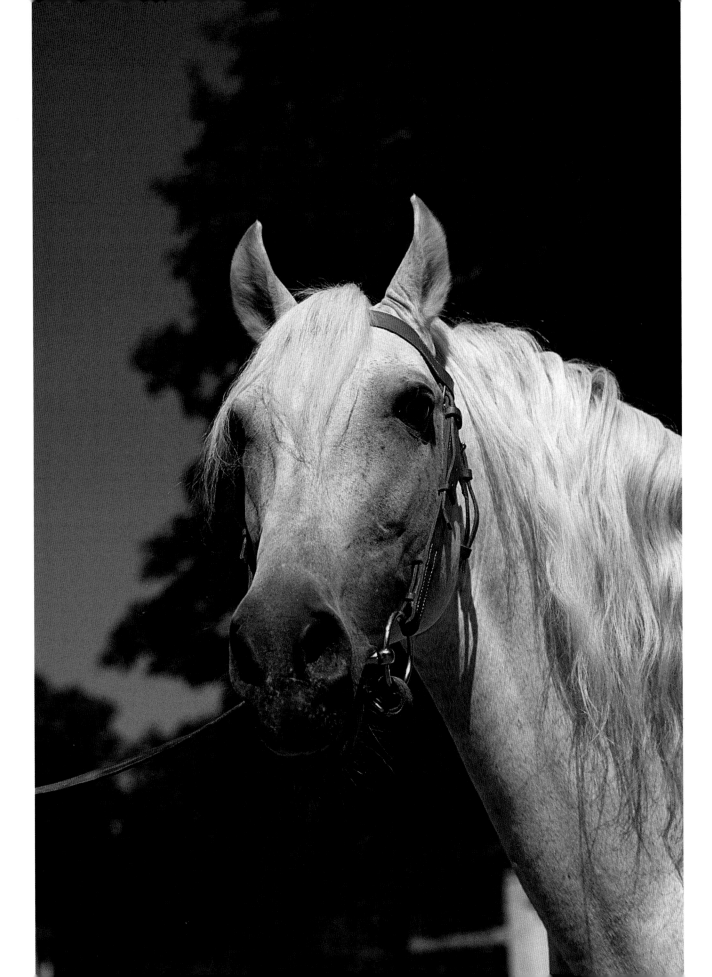

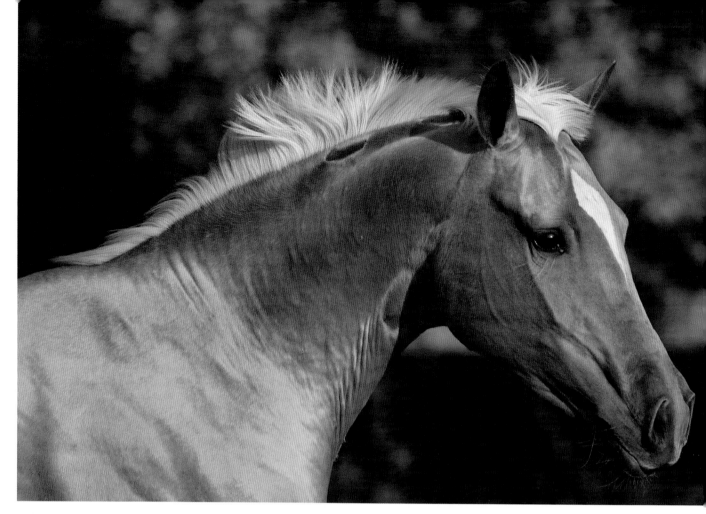
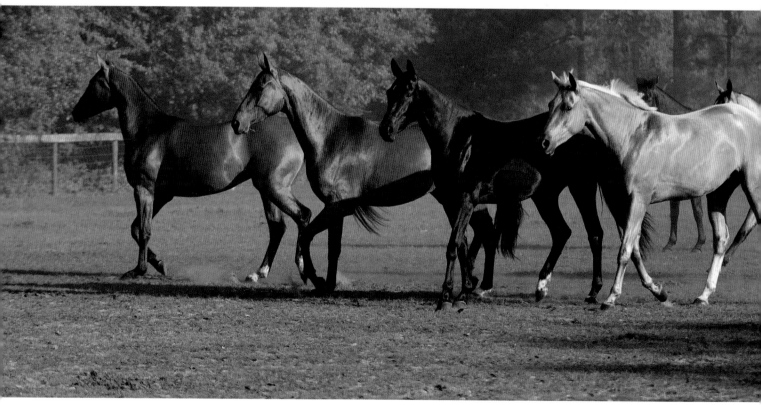

Akhal-Teke

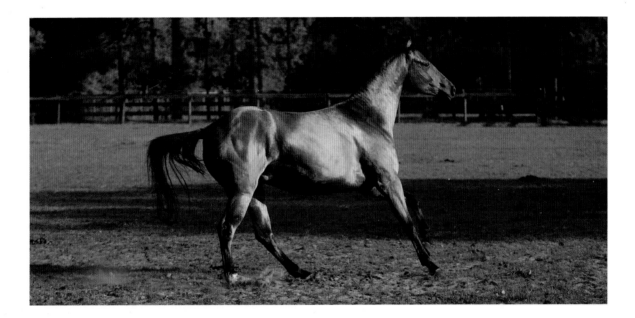

There is some debate as to whether the Akhal-Teke, the shining golden horse of Turkmenistan, predates the Arab. Skeletal remains of tall, fine-boned horses discovered in the southern part of the country date back to 2400BC. The breed shares similarities with the Arab, although its profile is straight rather than dished. Like the Arab, it has great powers of endurance as well as speed.

The breed takes its name from the Turkmen tribe called the Teke, who lived in the Akhal oasis in the challenging and unforgiving Kara Kum Desert in what was once the kingdom of Persia. The tribe was protected by the Caspian Sea to the west, mountains to the south and desert to the north. As a result of these factors, its prized equines were shielded from outside influence. The tribesmen held their horses in high regard, supplementing their diet with grains and animal fats whenever grass was scarce, and blanketing them against the freezing desert night.

Turkmenistan was annexed by Russia in the 1880s. The Russians called the horses *argamaks*, or 'tall and refined'. Under Russian auspices, the first Akhal-Teke stud was founded near Askhabad, the capital of Turkmenistan. The stallion Boinou was the progenitor of the dominant Akhal-Teke lines that are in use today.

Opposite top The Akhal-Teke shares its elegant bone structure with the Arab, but some believe it predates this breed.

Opposite below Most solid colours can be found in the Akhal-Teke, although grey is comparatively uncommon.

Above The characteristic iridescent sheen of the Akhal-Teke's coat adds to its beauty.

Sorraia

A Portuguese zoologist named Ruy d'Andrade is credited with not only discovering the Sorraia, but also recognizing its significance in modern horse breeds and saving it from extinction. He found the breed in the 1920s in the lowlands where two rivers, the Sor and the Raia, merge in southern Iberia, in what is now known as Portugal.

At first glance the Sorraia may appear somewhat unprepossessing: small and always dun, or *grullo* (greyish-dun), with a long, plain head and 'primitive' markings. Scientifically it is similar in type to the now-extinct Tarpan and was found to maintain wild behaviour, indicating that it had never been domesticated. It also has commonalities with the North African Barb, which can be explained by the fact that there was once a land bridge between Iberia and Africa, and with the Lusitano and Andalusian, of whom d'Andrade believed it was a predecessor.

Even though the Sorraia stands at little more than 14hh, it is considered to be a horse rather than a pony. (The term 'pony' is often used to define equines that measure under around 14hh, and that are more stocky in build than a horse, but the definition varies depending on context.) The Sorraia was undoubtedly among the stock taken to the New World by the Spanish conquistadors, and is the source of the *grullo* colouring that is still apparent in American breeds. Ruy d'Andrade realized that the Sorraia was in danger of extinction and acquired seven mares with which to start his own herd. Although the Sorraia still remains endangered, preservation programmes remain in force today.

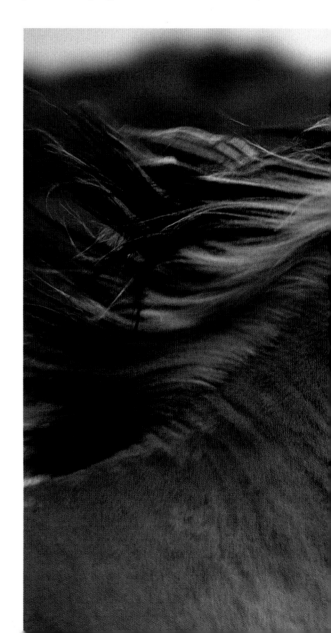

Opposite top Although the Sorraia has many 'pony' traits it is generally regarded as a small horse.

Right The Sorraia's relatively large head is set on a long and slender neck. Its mane and tail are bi-coloured, with lighter coloured hairs fringing the outsides of the longer growing black hairs.

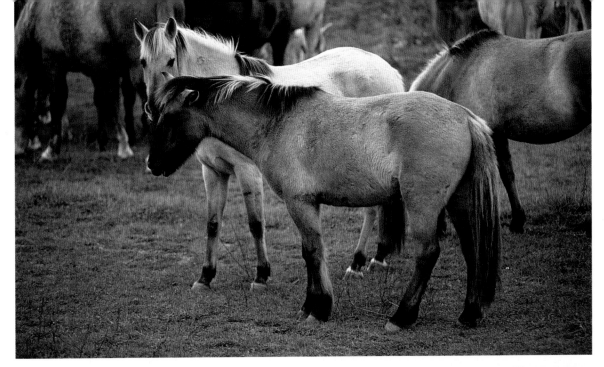

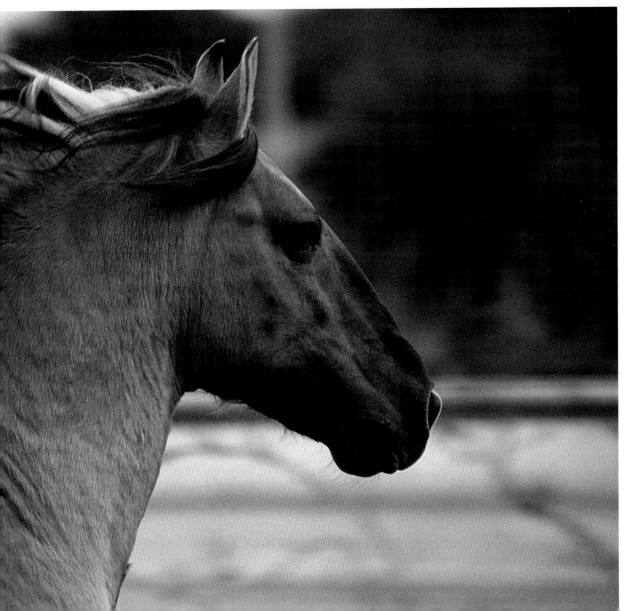

PRE/Iberian

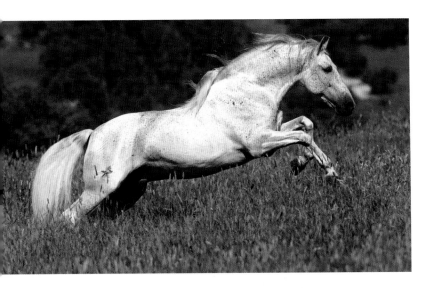

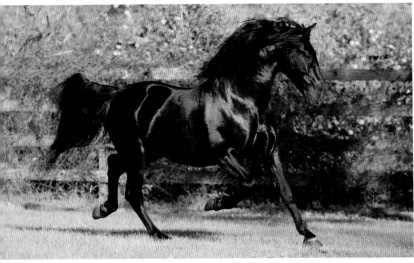

The Andalusian and its close cousin, the Lusitano, are now known collectively as the *Pura Raza Española* (PRE, or Pure Spanish Horse). An ancient breed and one of the few that is not influenced by the Arab, it is believed by some to have been the first horse breed to be tamed and ridden by humans. Indeed, cave paintings discovered on the Spanish peninsula, depicting horses being led by a man, date back to thousands of years BC.

It is thought that the Iberian horses descended from the rather unprepossessing native Spanish horse, the Sorraia – which in turn perhaps has roots in Przewalski's Horse and the Tarpan, as well as the Spanish Barb. They were the preferred war mounts of the Spanish conquistadors, Julius Caesar, Hannibal and Richard I.

The PRE was to fall out of favour as sleeker equines became more preferable for hunting and racing in the 1700s. The Andalusian was almost lost altogether, but the Carthusian monks, whose monastery was located high in the mountains of Spain, continued to breed this enchanting creature. Recognizing both the beauty of the breed and its rarity, the Spanish government placed a 100-year embargo on export of the Andalusian. When the ban was lifted in the 1960s, the world rediscovered the glory of the *Pura Raza Española*.

Top The PRE combines great beauty and sensitivity with strength and stamina. Its coat colour is most commonly grey.

Above The breed has a noble profile, strong, compact body and well-made limbs. It stands at around 16hh.

Opposite The PRE's elegant head, with small, neat ears and a large, kind eye, is set on a long, arched neck that is particularly well crested in stallions. The breed's mane and tail are long and thick.

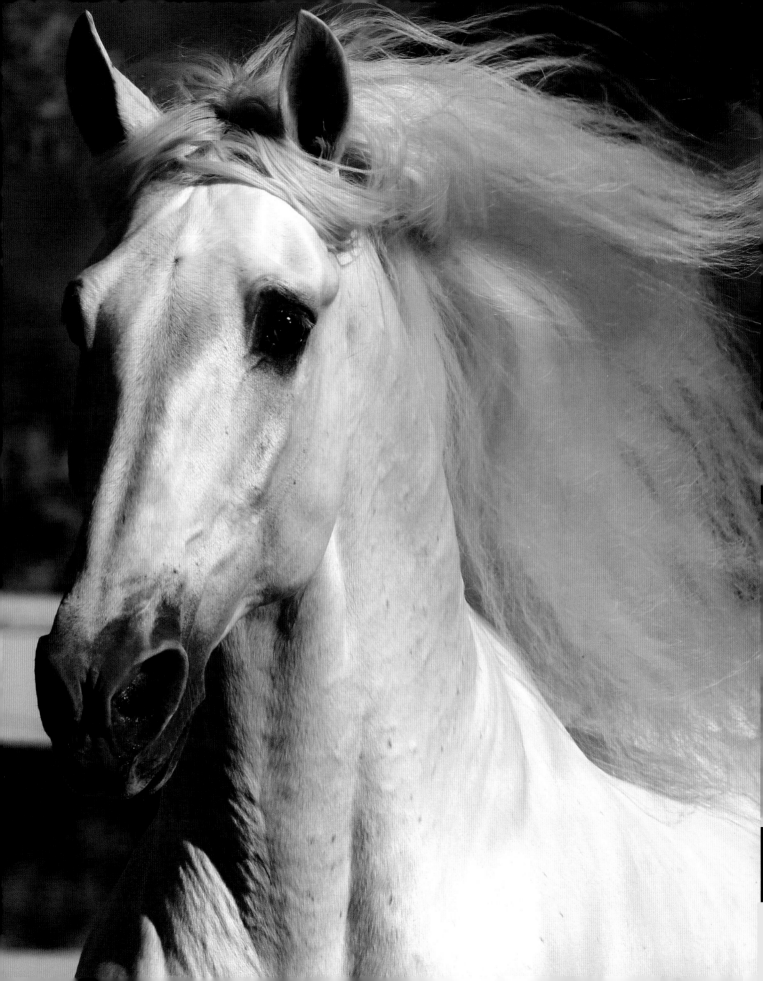

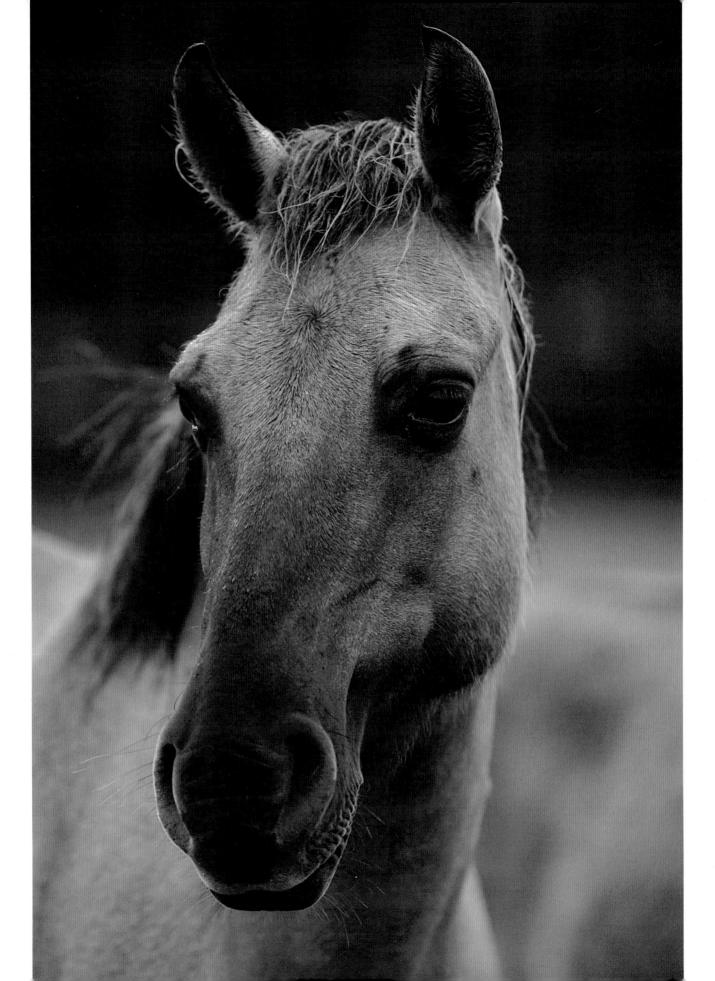

Tarpan/Konik

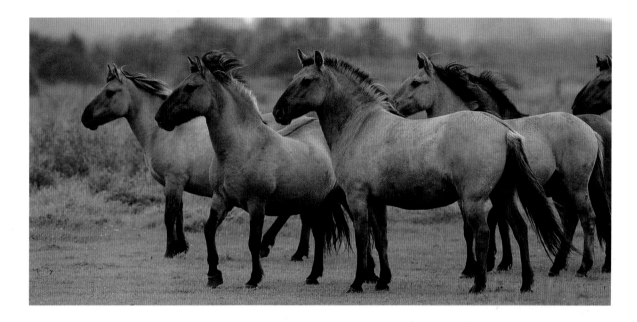

The Tarpan, a primitive creature also known as the Eurasian Wild Horse, has been extinct since the beginning of the 20th century. Prehistoric cave drawings tell us that a wild horse existed in southern France and Spain from around 3000BC. Artefacts indicate that the horse roamed as far as southern Russia, where it was domesticated by nomads. The Tarpan died out in the wild in around 1890, and the last horse in captivity died in 1909. Its closest living relative is the Polish Konik, which is thought to descend from the Tarpan that roamed wild in the forests of Poland. The Polish word *konik* translates as 'small horse', and the breed is certainly more horse than pony.

Attempts have been made, with some success, to reproduce the Tarpan using Konik, Przewalski's Horse, Swedish Gotland and Icelandic blood. German zoologists Heinz and Lutz Heck created a small equine that looked very similar to the Tarpan in 1933; the offspring of subsequent matings were sometimes referred to as 'Heck Horses'.

In 1936 Polish university professor Tadeusz Vetulani began a programme using Konik horses. Following this the Polish government created a preserve for the horses at Bialowieza. Over time the herd has developed more and more Tarpan traits, and the breed is now also known as the Polish Primitive Horse.

Opposite The Polish Konik shares many characteristics with the ancient Tarpan, which it has been used to recreate. Its head is large but in proportion to its frame, and it tends to be rather coarse, set on a short and powerful neck.

Above The Konik stands at around 13hh but is not considered to be a pony – its Polish name translates as 'small horse'. It is mouse-dun or *grullo* in colour, with a darker face and legs, a dark dorsal stripe and a semi-erect mane.

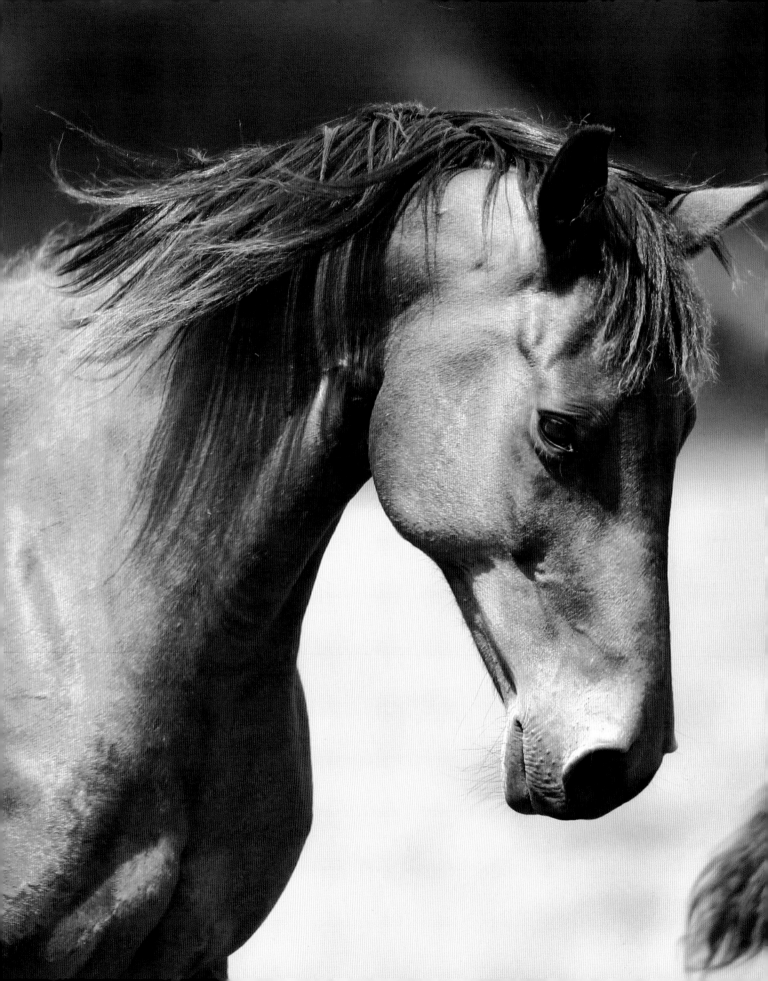

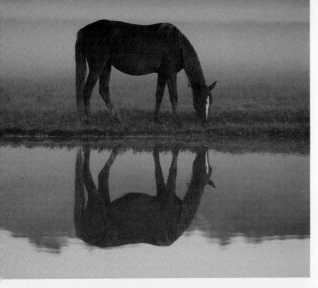

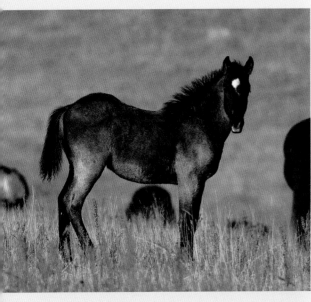

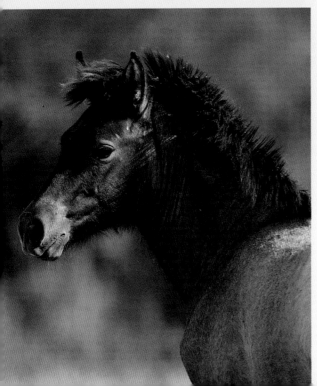

Wild and feral

The only truly wild horse is Przewalski's Horse, a separate subspecies from all other horses in existence today (page 7). Most 'wild' breeds now are actually feral; that is, they had been domesticated but were then returned to the wild. Perhaps the best-known feral breed is the iconic American Mustang.

Clockwise from far left Brumby (page 46); Chincoteague (page 40); Nokota (page 44); Camargue (page 38).

Przewalski's Horse

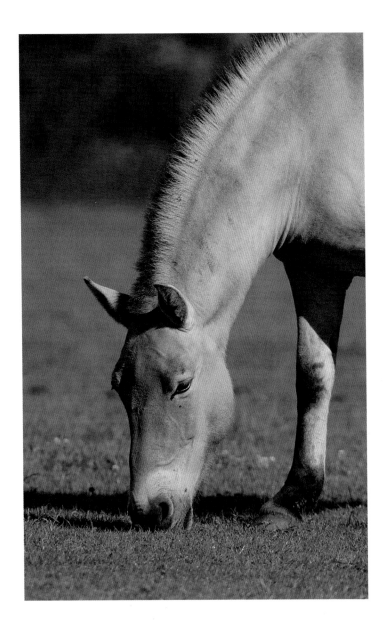

Also known as the Asiatic Wild Horse, this chunky little creature could perhaps be described as the 'missing link' between the Dawn Horse of prehistoric times and the equines we know today. The last horse to be found genuinely wild, as opposed to feral, Przewalski's Horse has 66 chromosomes – all other equine breeds have 64. If crossed with another breed, the offspring has 65 chromosomes. Subsequent matings produce a horse with 64 chromosomes that bears little resemblance to Przewalski's Horse.

When Colonel Nikolai Przewalski, a Polish explorer and geographer of Central and Eastern Asia, announced in the late 19th century that he had heard of wild horses in Mongolia, he caused a sensation. On his second foray to Central Asia, he brought back the skull and hide of a wild horse. On his third he saw herds of the animals in the Tachin Schara Nuru Mountains on the edge of the Gobi Desert. According to custom, the horse was named after the colonel, but it is believed that earlier explorers actually discovered it. A Scotsman wrote a description of animals that sound compellingly like Przewalski's Horse in a work published in the 1700s, and an even earlier reference appears in a manuscript published in 1427. The horse was extinct in the wild until the mid-1990s, when – through the efforts of the Przewalski Foundation – two breeding groups were reintroduced to Mongolia.

Above The erect brushy mane of Przewalski's Horse is a typical 'primitive' trait.

Opposite top The pale 'mealy' muzzle of this horse can also be seen in Britain's Exmoor pony, which had been isolated for centuries.

Opposite below Although Przewalski's Horse rarely stands taller than 13hh it is regarded as a horse rather than a pony.

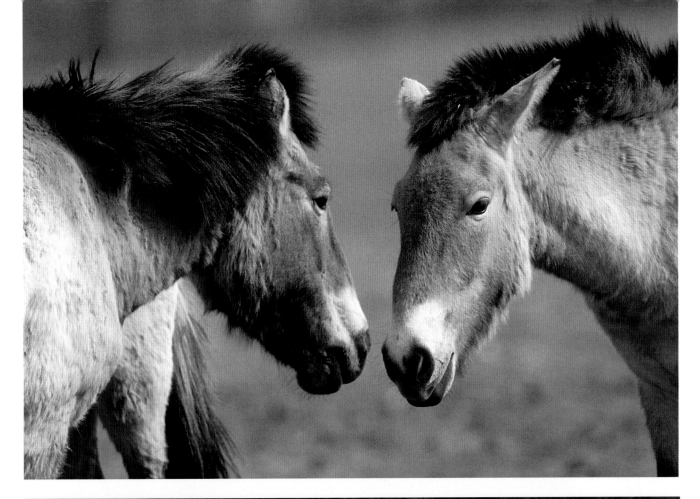
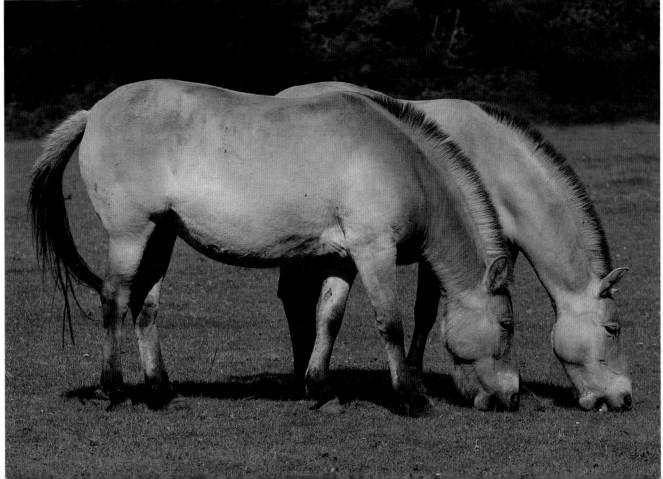

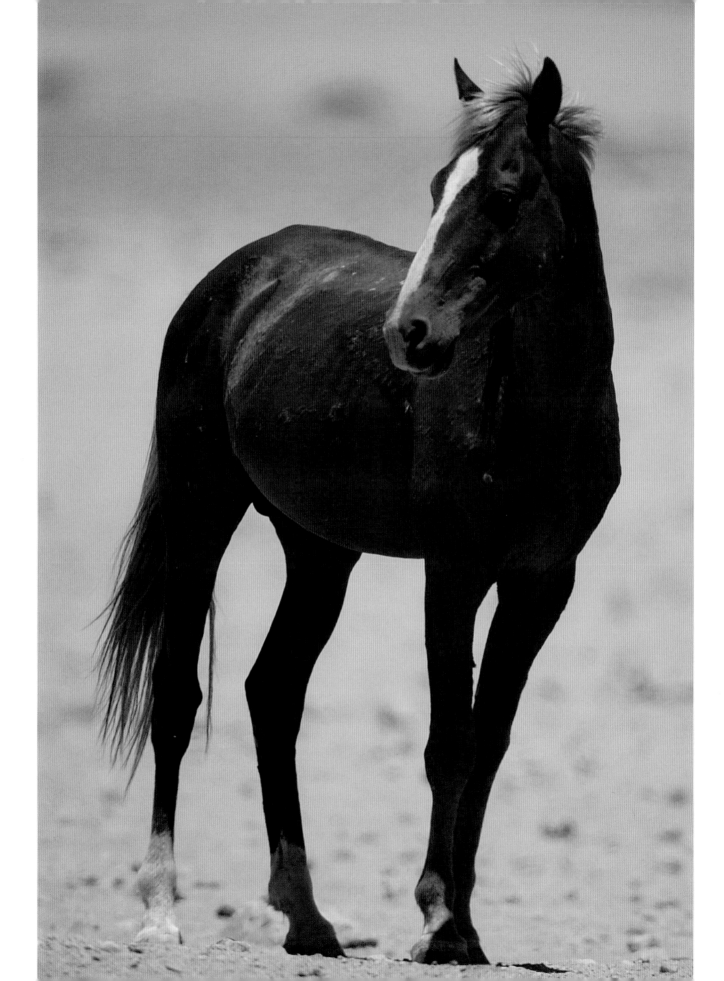

Namib Desert Horse

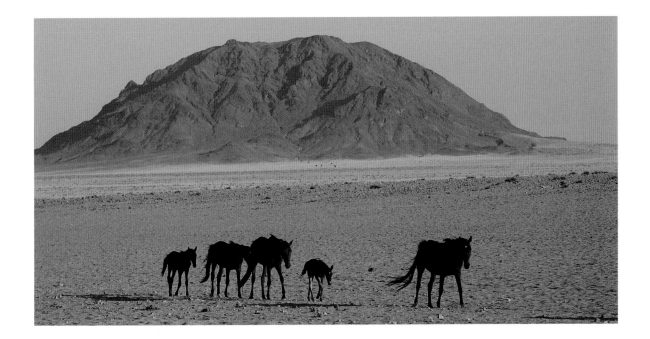

Rather less than 150 of these athletic equines of unknown origin live in an area covering about 135 square miles in the Namib Desert in south-west Angola. Horses are not indigenous to the area and they are thought to be feral, not truly wild. They are uniquely isolated, and their harsh environment has resulted in the survival of only the fittest individuals.

A plausible theory is that the horses were originally brought to the desert during the German occupation of south-west Africa. It is known that an eccentric German nobleman, Baron Hans-Heinrich von Wolf, set up a horse-breeding station in the veldt. When he was called up to fight in the First

World War there was no one left to tend to the horses, and herds of them then ran wild. It may be that some wandered about 90 miles south-west to Garub, at the edge of the Namib Desert. On the other hand, the horses could equally have originated from mounts of a South African expedition that took control of the Luderitz-Keetmanshoop railway line during the war. Whatever their origins, Namib Desert Horses have adapted to their environment. They are constantly on the move to avoid predators and, unlike most horse breeds, are able to survive for a long time without water – said to be up to 72 hours. They are worthy of wonder and admiration.

Opposite The lean, muscular and strong-boned frame of the Namib Desert Horse is typical of the hotblooded 'desert' type, though the breed's origins are uncertain.

Above The Namib Desert Horse generally lives in breeding groups numbering up to ten horses. These comprise one or two stallions plus mares and foals, which are led by a mare.

Camargue

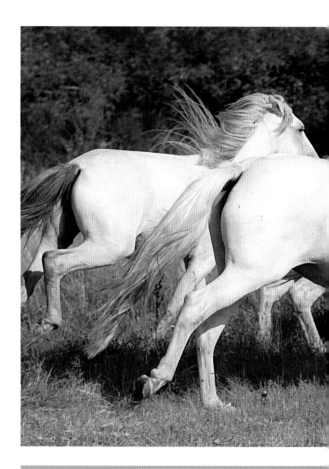

Horses have existed in the harsh wetlands at the mouth of France's River Rhone for thousands of years. Ghostlike with their almost pure white coats, these hardy creatures survive on the tough marsh grass of the Rhone delta. They are named Camargue for the region, but are also known as the 'horses of the sea'.

The Camargue very rarely stands much above 14.3hh at maturity, but has more horse than pony characteristics. Its exact origins are unknown, but cave drawings of horses in the area date back to some 15,000BC. Equine bones discovered in the region are thought to be even more ancient.

The hardy Camargue is held in high regard. In 1976 the French government registered all breeders, and a representative visits each herd for an annual *marguage*, or branding. Foals born within the defined Camargue region are registered as *sous berceau*, and those born outside as *hors berceau* (out of the birth place). Once prized as cavalry mounts, Camargues are used by the *gardien* – French cowboys – to herd the black bulls of the region, which are every bit as tough as the horses themselves.

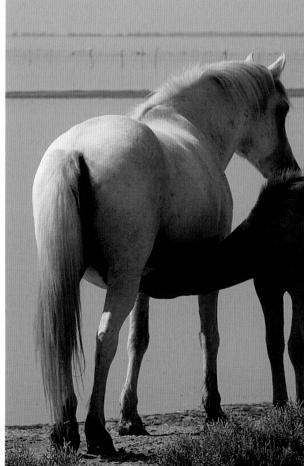

Right A Camargue mare and her foal in the wetlands of the Rhone delta – the foal's coat will lighten to grey.

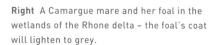

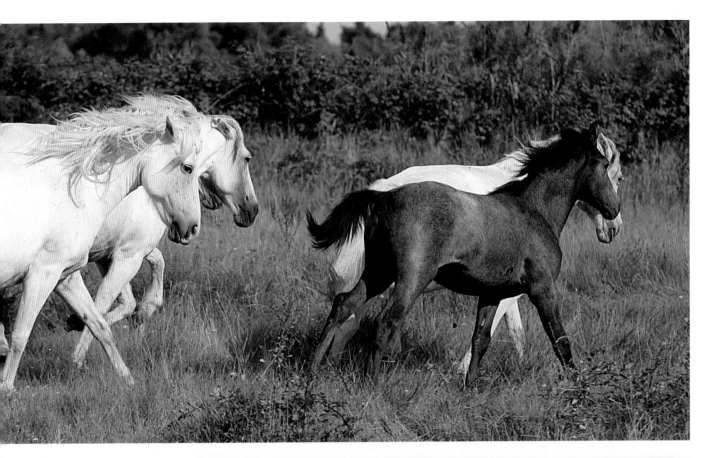

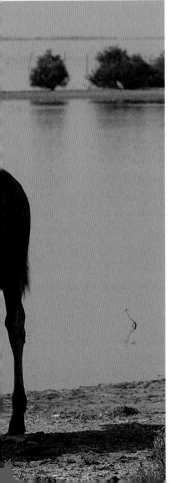

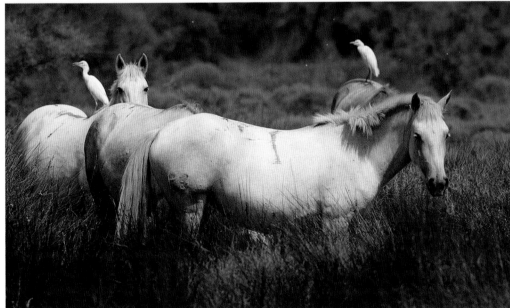

Top The hardy little Camargue is capable of enduring bad weather and long periods with little food. Its strong legs and hard feet allow it to travel long distances.

Above With its infallible instinct and broad, steady hooves, the Camargue is perfectly adapted to its watery environment.

Chincoteague

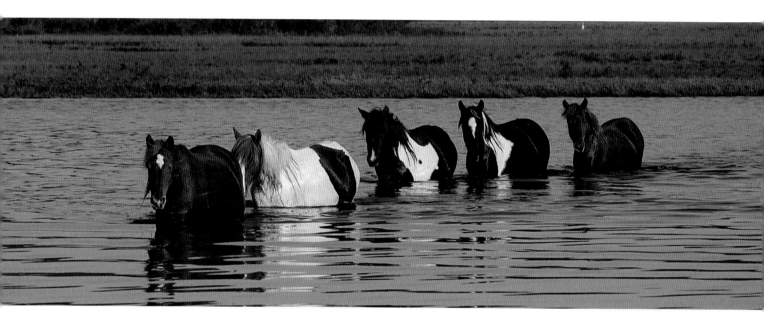

Immortalized in Marguerite Henry's well-known book *Misty of Chincoteague*, published in 1947, these feral ponies actually live on the neighbouring island of Assateague, off the coast of Virginia and Maryland in the United States, rather than on Chincoteague (meaning 'beautiful land across the sea'). It is not known how the horses came to live on Assateague; romantics have it that they were shipwrecked from a Spanish galleon in the 17th century and swam to shore, but this is probably more myth than truth.

Settlers in Virginia found it a pleasing place to live, with fertile soil, a temperate climate and the sea providing an endless source of food. By the late 1600s some of them had relocated to Chincoteague, which was a more hospitable place than the larger Assateague. The wild horses of Assateague would swim across the narrow channel to Chincoteague and lay waste to farmers' crops. Soon the horses were being domesticated by the islanders, who swam them across the channel. This proved beneficial for both human and horse – the horses were hardy, intelligent workers, and a selection process resulted in control of the herd, which did not become too big for the island. The ponies are still swum between the islands each year for the annual 'pony penning', held to monitor and protect the Chincoteague herds.

Above The feral horses living on Assateague and Chincoteague are used to swimming between these islands.

Opposite Chincoteagues are hardy and 'good doers', able to obtain sustenance from the most meagre grazing.

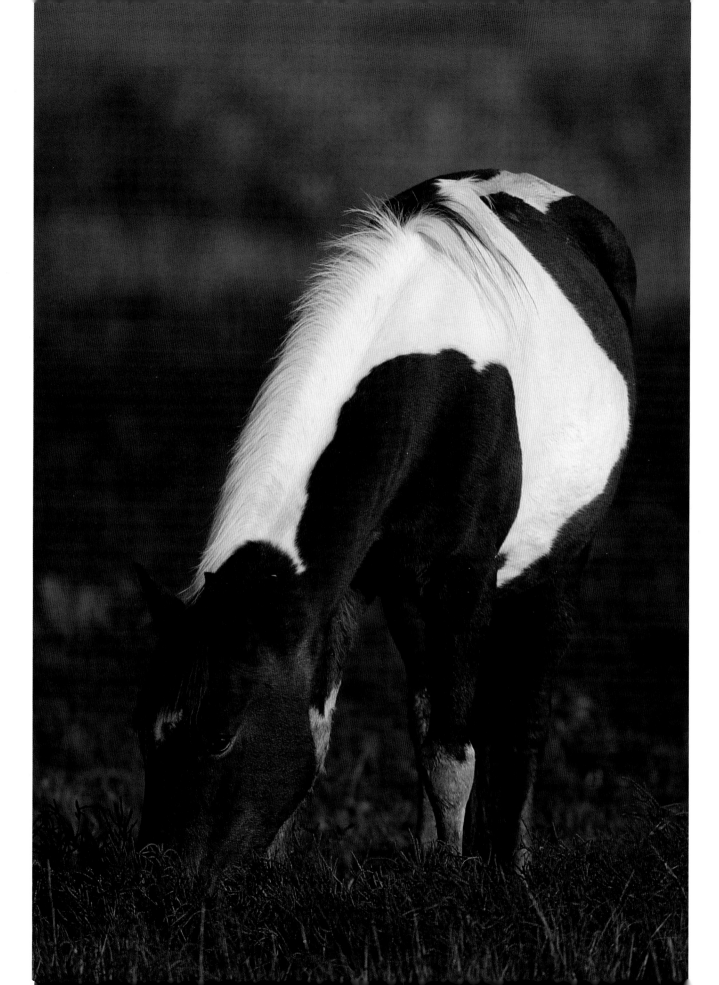

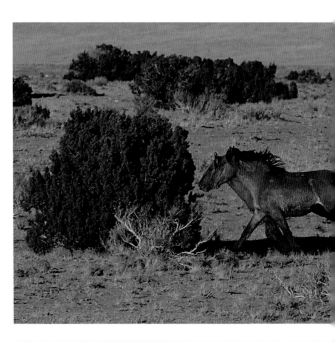

Mustang

If any horse were an icon it must surely be the American Mustang, made famous in countless books, films and television shows. It is feral rather than wild, and descended from the Spanish stock imported to the New World in the 16th century. Before then there were no horses in the Americas for at least 10,000 years. Skirmishes took place between the Spanish settlers and Native Americans, and the Spaniards were driven back and forced to leave their horses. Allowed to run free and breed at will, these equines were the first Mustangs. The name of the breed comes from the Spanish *mesteño*, which means 'stray animal'.

In the 1800s, as ranchers moved in and spread across the American plains, it was customary for the cowhands to set their horses loose at night and recapture them the following day. Mustangs were often simultaneously rounded up with these horses.

By 1900 there were an estimated two million Mustangs roaming free in North America. Deemed as a pest, they were indiscriminately slaughtered, often shot from aircraft (with varying degrees of accuracy) and poisoned. In 1971 the Wild and Free-Roaming Horses and Burros Act was introduced to protect America's favourite 'wild' horse.

Right The *grullo* colouring of the Mustang pictured on the right almost certainly comes from the Spanish Sorraia.

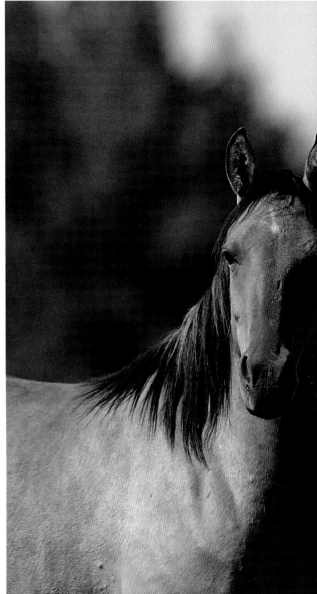

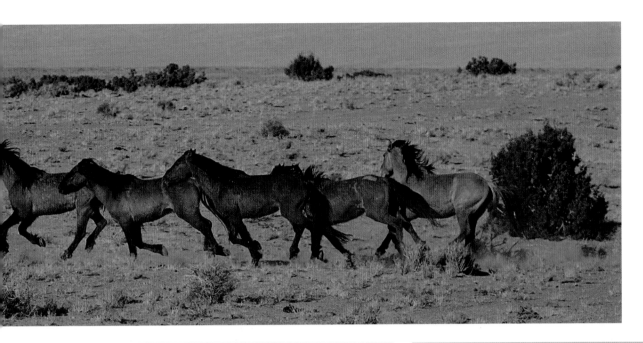

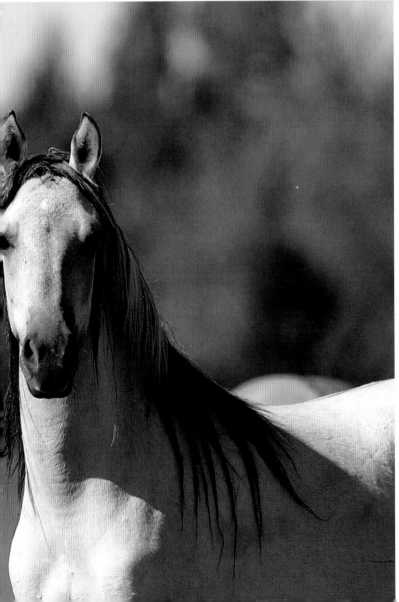

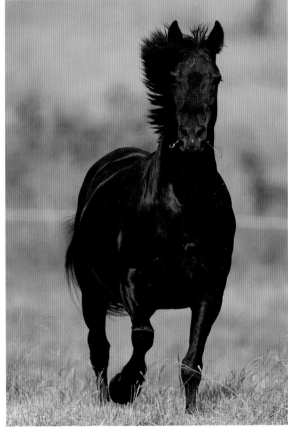

Top American icon: Mustangs gallop across the wide open spaces of Utah in the United States.

Above This Mustang mare shares many similarities with the PRE, the Spanish breed that was taken to America by Conquistadors.

Nokota

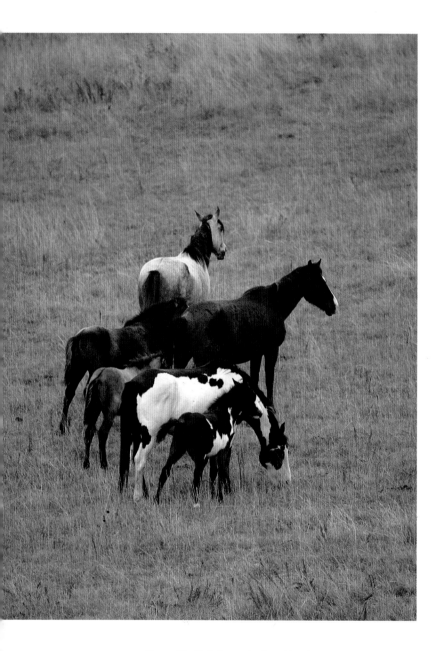

Feral horses once roamed the Dakotas of North America. The Nokota horse breed is descended from their last survivors, which had inhabited the rugged Little Missouri River Badlands of south-west North Dakota for at least a century. Theodore Roosevelt, who ranched in Little Missouri in 1883–6, wrote: 'In a great many localities there are wild horses to be found, which, although invariably of domestic descent… are yet quite as wild as the antelope on whose range they have intruded.'

The Nokota is closely related to the Mustang and has the same Spanish origins, but was influenced by other breeds. In the early 19th century, North Dakota was part of a huge intercontinental network linked by the Missouri river. French and English fur traders based in Canada were part of this network, and horses were a valuable commodity. It is likely that the bigger Canadian horses – developed using imported French breeds – had some influence on the wild herds. Sitting Bull of Little Bighorn fame rode horses that were noticeably more rangy in type than the usual Spanish Mustang that was favoured by the Native Americans.

When the Theodore Roosevelt National Park was created in the 1950s, some of the wild horses were fenced in by accident. The National Park Service spent decades trying to rid the park of the horses, until local horsemen Frank and Leo Kuntz began to buy them to save them from slaughter, naming them Nokotas.

Above The Nokota can be found in a large variety of colours, shapes and sizes. The typical Spanish colourings of dun, roan and overo (white over dark body markings) are seen in the breed.

Opposite top The height of the Nokota varies considerably. It has a square-set, angular frame with prominent withers, sloped croup and strong legs and hooves.

Opposite bottom The grey-dun colour known as *grullo* can be found in the Nokota as well as the Mustang.

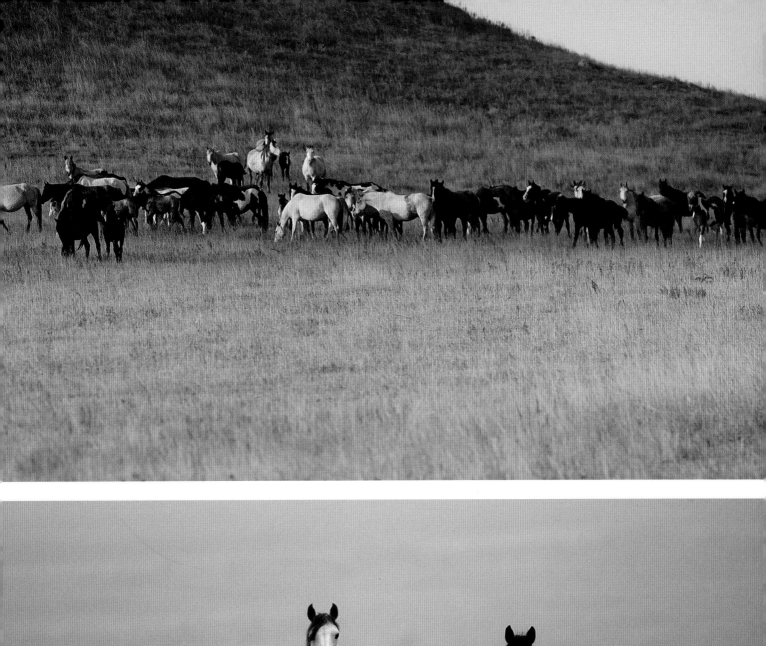
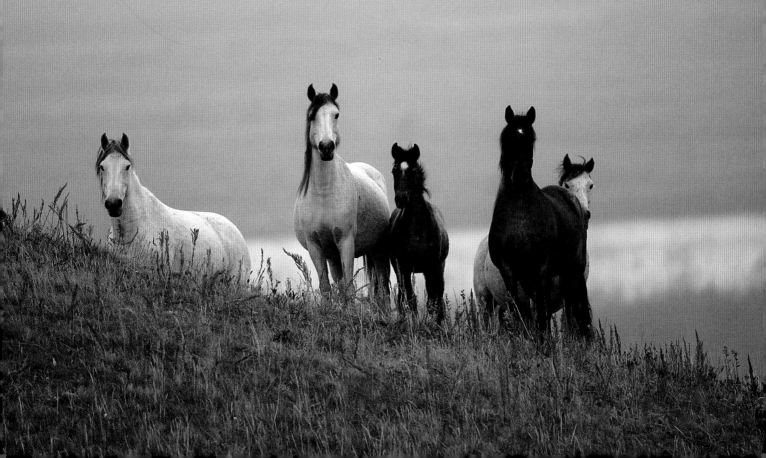

Brumby

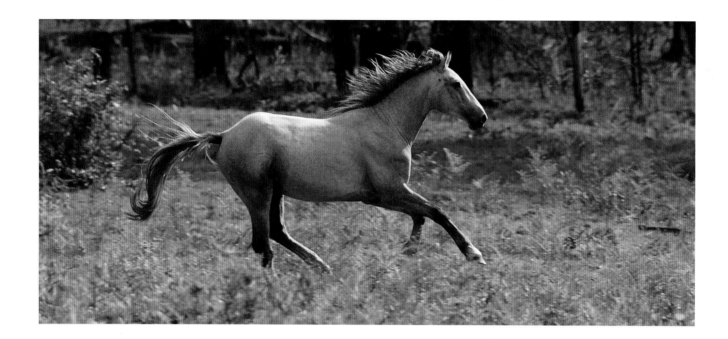

If America's Mustang is her iconic horse, the Brumby is Australia's. Like the Mustang, the Brumby is a mix of breeds of domesticated horse that were either set free or escaped and were permitted to roam, unchecked, across the Northern Territory, South-east Australia and Queensland.

The earliest settlers to the Australian continent brought horses with them in 1788; these included British pony and draught breeds, as well as Arabs and Thoroughbreds. There is some debate about the origin of the name 'Brumby'. Some believe that several horses were left behind by a Sergeant James Brumby when he moved from New South Wales to Tasmania in 1804. When someone enquired as to whom the equines belonged, the reply was: 'They're Brumby's.' The name may equally have derived from the Aboriginal word for 'wild', *baroomby*, or from Baramba, the name of a cattle station in Queensland.

Because the horses live largely unchecked, they are of varying quality. The population is estimated at around 400,000, but in temperate seasons can increase by as much as 20 per cent a year. Many see the feral herds as pests that compete with livestock for food and water, but to others they are a much-loved symbol of Australia and part of her valuable tourist industry.

Above Even though the Brumby is feral rather than wild, it is generally considered untameable, with an uneven temper.

Opposite top Brumbies are found all over Australia and tend to travel in small herds or 'bands', often consisting of a stallion, his mares and young stock.

Opposite below All shapes, sizes and colours can be seen in the Brumby, and its quality varies considerably.

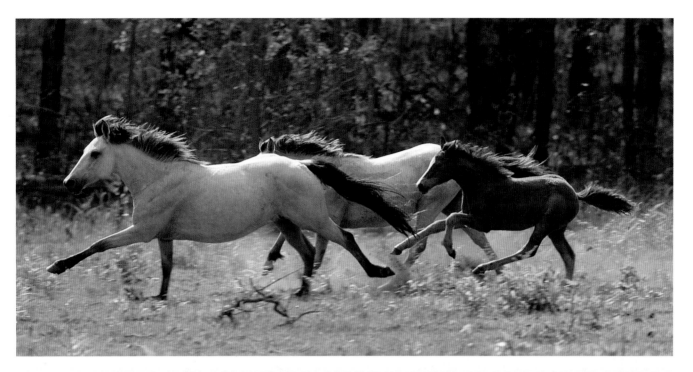
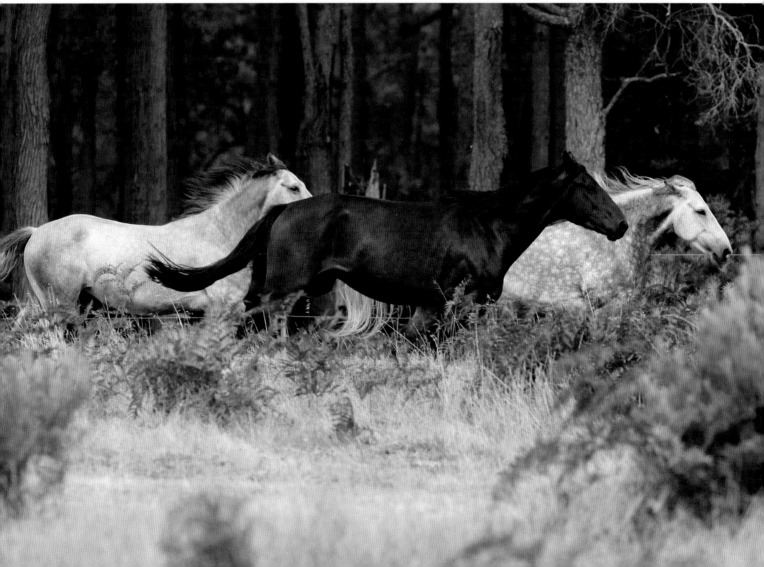

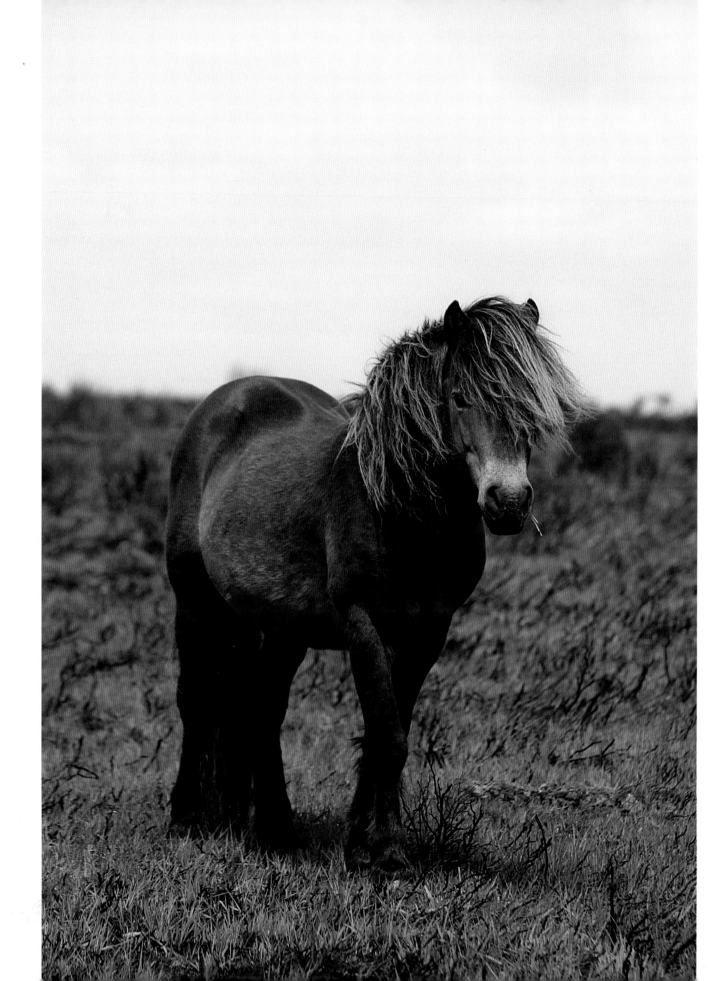

Exmoor

Desolate and wild, south-west England's moors are unforgiving places to survive in. Despite this, the Exmoor pony has adapted supremely to its challenging environment. Wild equines have existed in Britain for at least 100,000 years, after crossing the marshy land that was later to become the English Channel. When the Channel formed around 7,000 years ago, the horses were trapped on the islands. While other British ponies were subjected to outside influences as various breeds were brought to the mainland, the ponies on Exmoor were isolated and remained pure.

Exmoor itself was for centuries a royal hunting ground. When it was sold off in 1818, the last royal warden, Sir Thomas Acland, took 30 Exmoor ponies to enable him to breed his own herd, and other farmers did the same. Sir Thomas devoted his time to breeding true-to-type Exmoor ponies. These were to form the famous Anchor herd whose bloodlines continue in the modern breed.

The Exmoor suffered badly during the Second World War, when its eponymous home was used as a training ground for troops, who used the ponies for target practice. At one time there were just 30 ponies left on the moor. Today the breed remains listed as 'critical' by the Rare Breeds Survival Trust, but efforts are being made by conservation societies to ensure that it lives on for generations to come.

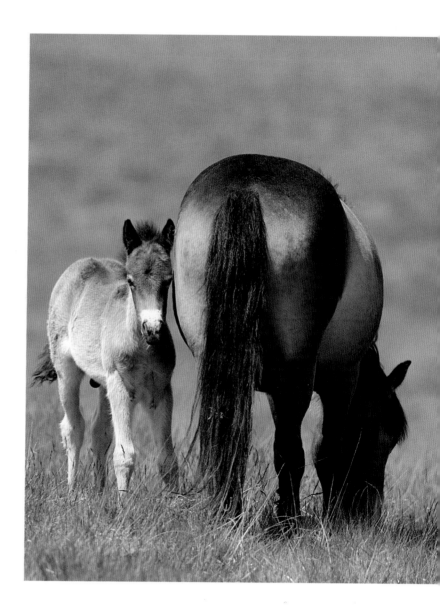

Opposite The Exmoor has a thick thatch of mane and tail. These and its short stature – around 12.3hh – protect it from the wind.

Above This charming foal already has the typical 'mealy' muzzle of the Exmoor pony.

Mérens

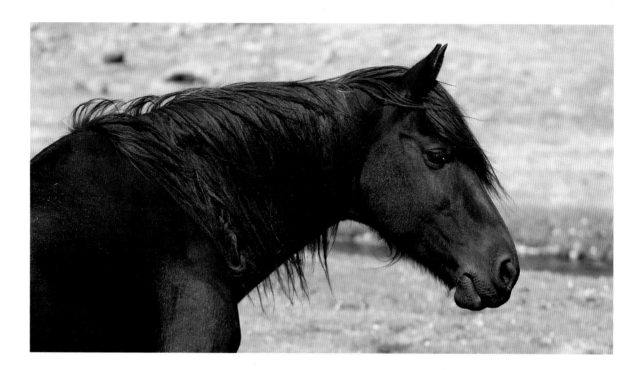

Paintings of equines remarkably similar to the Mérens are found on the walls of the world-famous Grotte de Niaux, the cave in the foothills of the Pyrenees in south-west France that dates back to 17,000–9000BC. This region of France is called Ariège, and the Mérens is sometimes known as the Ariegeois pony. The name Mérens comes from a village high in the mountains called Mérens-les-Vals, near Andorra.

Although it stands at no more than 14.2hh, the Mérens pony was used as a cavalry mount both during the Middle Ages and by Napoleon during his Russian campaign, as well as by the *montagnol*, or mountain farmer. An easy keeper, the Mérens is hard working and docile, although it can be stubborn.

Horse breeders in Ariège leave their animals out all year and turn them away into the mountains for rest and recuperation on the summer pastures, so that the Mérens returns to a natural herd existence. The pony is always black (although its winter coat has a reddish cast), and it resembles the British Fell and Dales ponies. Prized for its endurance, it has been exported all over Europe – one was gifted to the former British Prime Minister Tony Blair.

Above The Mérens has a calm and docile temperament and is an easy keeper, able to thrive on short rations. It has a neat and pretty head with wide-set eyes, and a short and muscular neck. Mérens horses are very similar to each other, probably as a result of the breed's isolation.

Opposite top In early summer the horses are led up to the pastures in the high mountains, where they spend several months living free.

Opposite below Like the Friesian the Mérens is always black, suggesting a genetic connection between the breeds. It has a calm disposition, but will, like most horses, play fight with its peers.

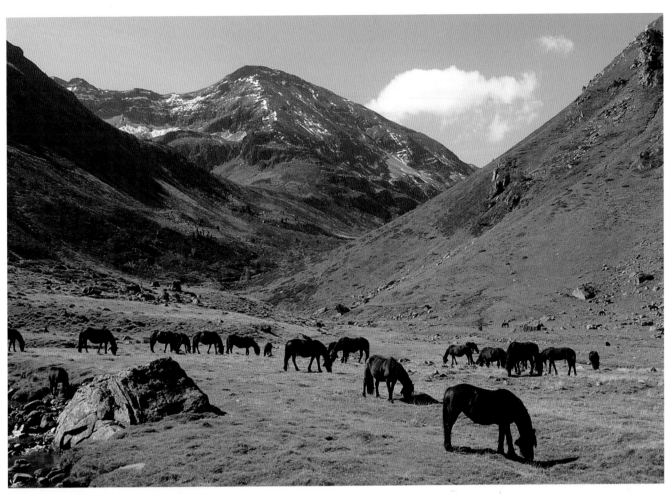

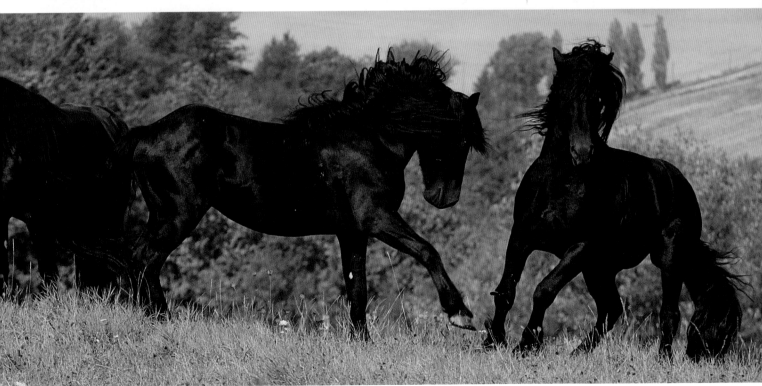

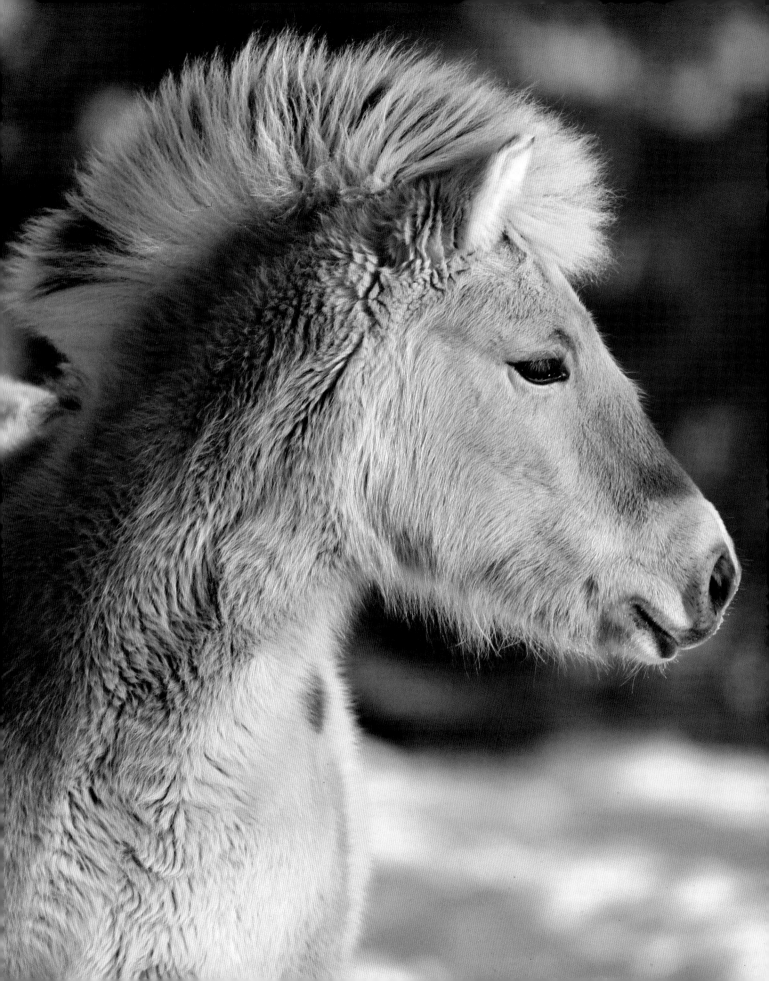

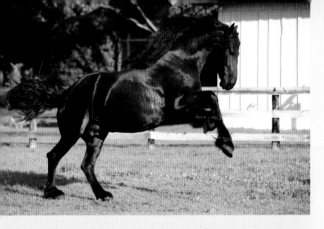
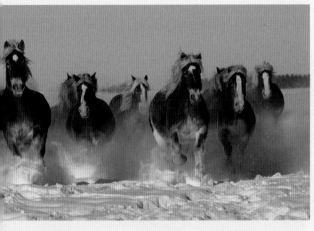
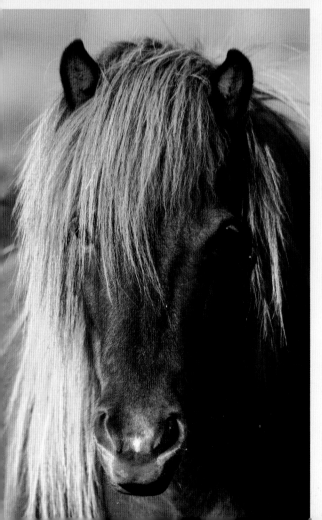

Europe

In equine terminology horses are broadly divided into coldblooded, hotblooded and warmblooded types (page 7). Coldbloods are relatively stable, calm, strong and rugged, and are often used as work horses. The ancient Diluvial Horse that roamed Europe was coldblooded. Hotbloods are sensitive and energetic, and many are used as race horses. The hotblooded Arab and Thoroughbred were used on native stock in Europe and produced the warmblood – which today is the ultimate equine athlete.

Clockwise from far left Fjord (page 68); Friesian (page 54); Belgian (page 74); Icelandic (page 71).

Friesian

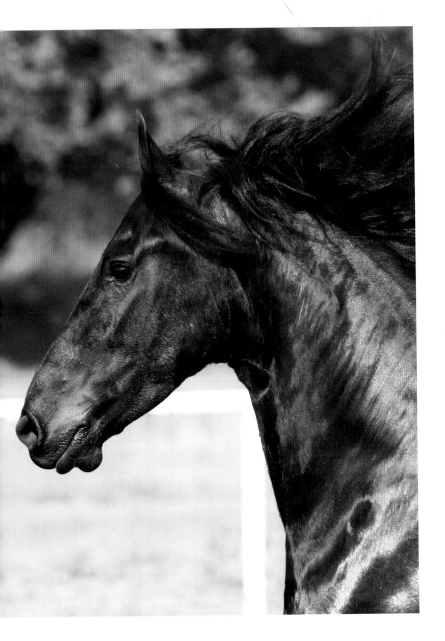

With the midnight sheen of a Raven's wing, the Friesian – named after the Dutch province of Friesland – is one of the most striking horse breeds. The only horse native to the Netherlands, it has existed since at least the 13th century, although the *Friesch Paarden-Stamboek*, the breed's studbook, was not established until 1879.

Horses that looked remarkably similar to the modern Friesian are depicted in the iconography of the ancient world. At the start of the Christian era Friesian troops and their horses were documented in Britannia, and it is thought that the Friesian is the ancestor of Britain's mighty Shire, as well as her Fell and Dales pony breeds.

The Friesian fell out of favour when heavier breeds became more popular for agriculture, then later when mechanization took over in farming. Both these factors almost sounded the death knell for the Dutch black beauty. It was deemed to be too 'showy' for agriculture, and by 1913 there were just three studbook stallions left. The people of Friesland, however, rallied to save their native breed, and for a while its fortunes were reversed. By the mid-1960s its numbers had dropped again and there were just 500 breeding mares in existence. A campaign to resurrect the breed was introduced, largely by the national riding association, De Oosprong. By 2007 some 40,000 Friesians were registered. Today the breed is renowned for its noble beauty, versatility and affinity with humans.

Above The Netherlands' Friesian is one of the most striking of horse breeds, with a noble head and gleaming black coat.

Opposite Powerful and compact (it stands at around 15hh), the Friesian makes a smart carriage horse.

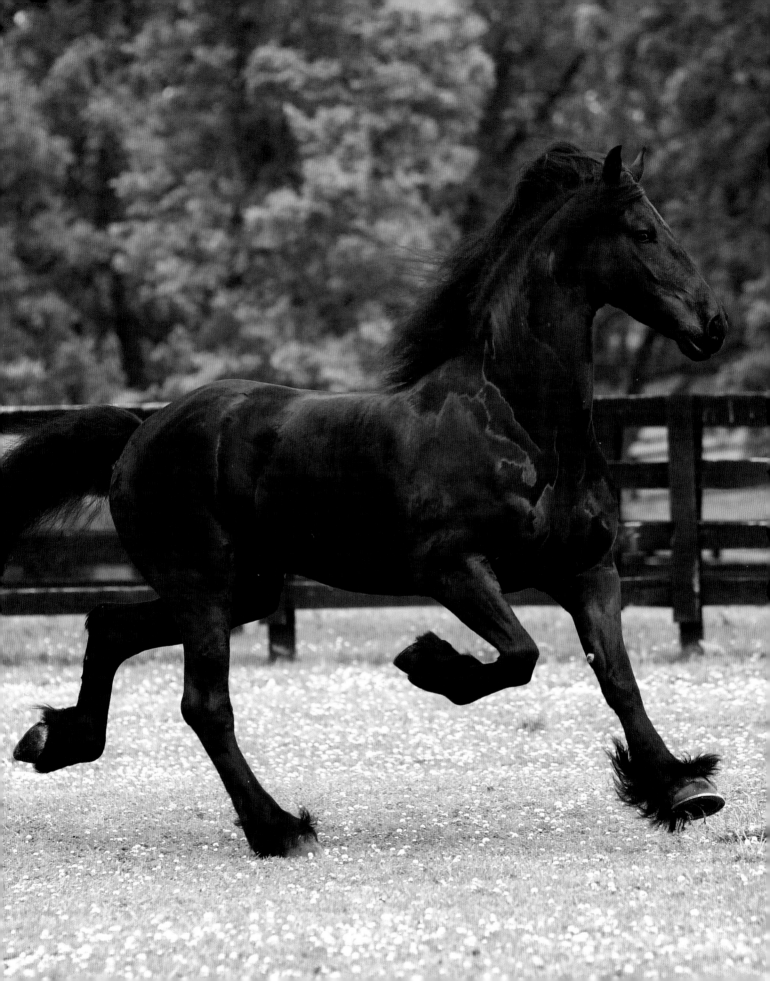

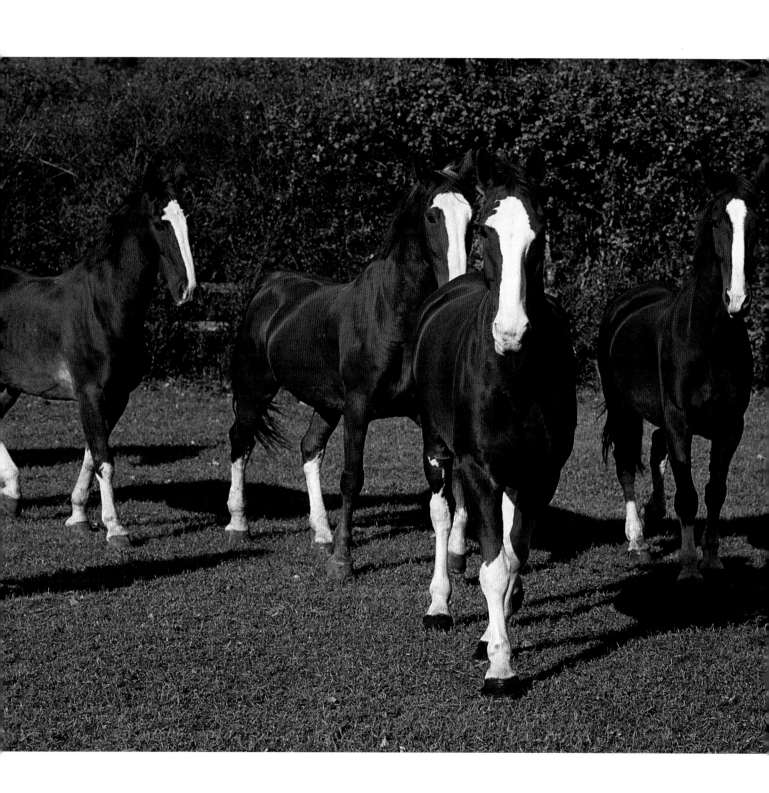

Gelderlander

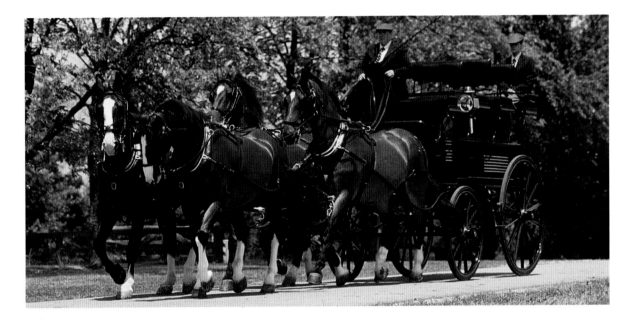

Originally bred to pull carriages in the Dutch province of Gelderland, where native mares were crossed with Andalusian, Norfolk Roadster, Neapolitan, Friesian and Holstein stallions, the Gelderlander is a 20th-century success story. The aim was to produce an all-round utility horse strong enough to work the land, smart enough to pull a carriage and comfortable enough to ride. Later infusions of Oldenburg, Thoroughbred and Hackney blood were introduced to refine the breed, which became sought after as a carriage horse because of its stylish gaits, made possible due to the Hackney influence. Although the Gelderlander is a warmblood breed its head tended to be rather plain, but it was generally attractive and had the sweet temper of the Friesian. In the early 1960s the VLN, which managed the studbook, opened a sports register, and Gelderlanders were crossed back to Thoroughbreds to lighten and further refine the breed. These part-breds became increasingly popular. They were also allowed to be registered as pure-bred Gelderlanders, so the breed became more diluted.

Together with the similar Groningen, bred in the northern Netherlands, the Gelderlander was used to establish the Dutch warmblood, a force to be reckoned with in all competitive disciplines. Although the studbook was closed, there are still breeders producing the true, pure Gelderlander.

Opposite These well-matched Gelderlanders would make a magnificent team of four for carriage driving.

Above The Gelderlander's excellent gaits and durability make it suitable for a variety of equestrian sports, particularly four-in-hand carriage driving.

Hanoverian

Germany's best-known warmblood is arguably her most successful export. The mighty Hanoverian is revered as a supreme competition horse the world over. Indeed, the breed was the choice of kings. King George II of England, who was also Elector of Hanover, founded the state stud at Celle in 1735 with the aim of breeding all-purpose workhorses and cavalry mounts. Holsteiner, English Thoroughbred, Cleveland Bay and Andalusian blood was used to refine local stock, and by the end of the 18th century the Hanoverian was highly regarded as a coach horse.

The first studbook was opened in 1888 and the Hanoverian became one of the most popular breeds in Europe. In 1922 the Verband Hannoverscher Warmblutzuchter (Society of Hanoverian Warmblood Breeders) was formed to represent more than 10,000 breeders and ensure the future of the breed. The horse is now in great demand in all competitive spheres, combining as it does good looks with great athleticism and a trainable disposition.

The Hanoverian's worldwide reputation is due to the breeders who were prepared to move with demand and produce the sort of horse equestrians want, as well as to maintain the best breeding stock through rigorous selection. Their aim was to create a noble, versatile warmblood with elastic, ground-covering gaits. Few would argue that they have indeed succeeded.

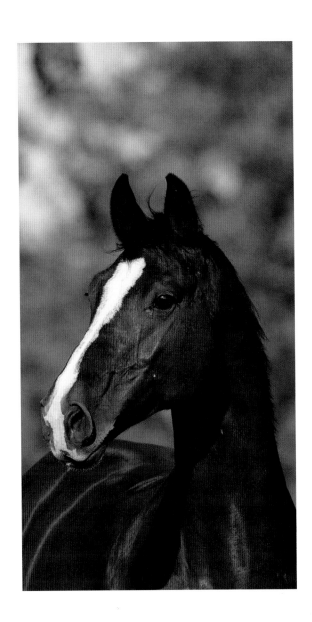

Above The Hanoverian is one of the most graceful of the warmblood breeds, with a handsome and noble head on a well-proportioned, well set-on neck.

Opposite This delightful foal shows off the paces and fine conformation that make the Hanoverian so popular worldwide.

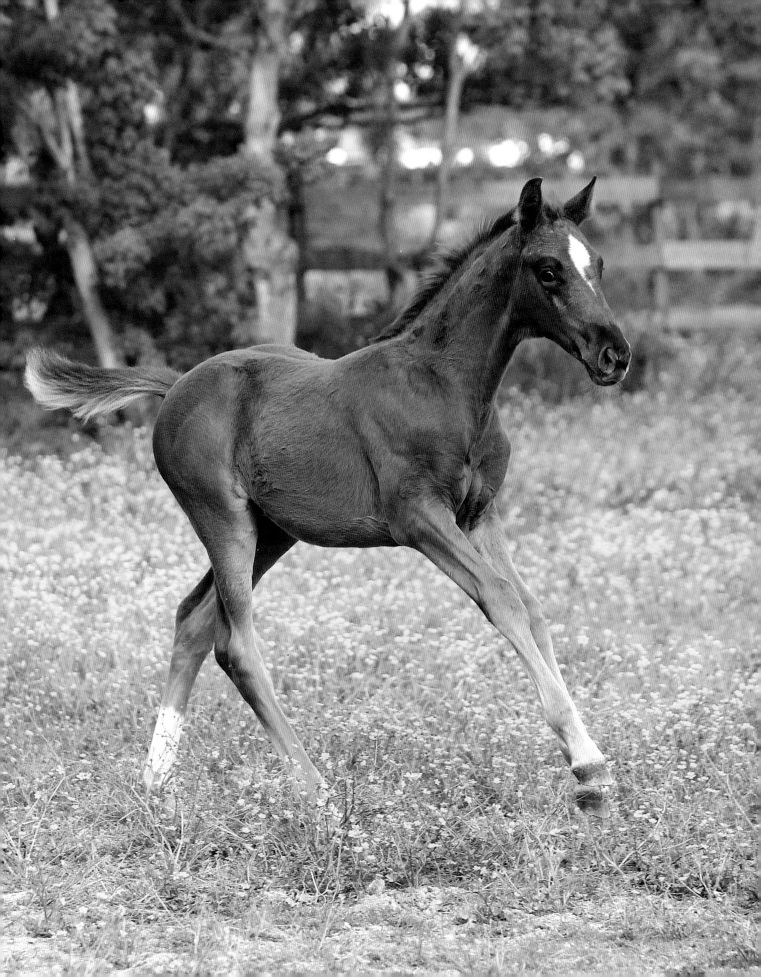

Trakehner

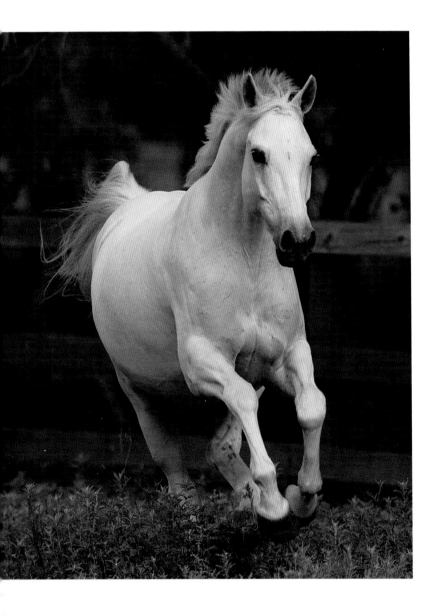

King Frederick the Great of Prussia decreed in 1732 that 'nothing but pure gold must be used for breeding' at the royal stud he established at Trakennen. He had admired the light but robust horses ridden by King Wilhelm I of Prussia and decided that his own army should be mounted on good-looking horses that were comfortable to ride, and could cover the ground quickly and stay sound. To this end, he merged seven of his royal breeding farms to form the Trakennen stud.

Invasion after the Second World War resulted in the decimation of the stud and its herds, and the breed was only saved by an historic journey known thereafter as 'The Trek'. The East Prussian people hitched their precious horses to wagons with all their belongings and trekked for 600 miles, driven mercilessly towards the Baltic Sea by the Soviet Army. Forced to cross the vast expanse of ice, many horses and people alike did not survive – only 1,000 horses out of an estimated 8,000 remained when the travellers reached the safety of West Germany. These were undoubtedly the toughest and most enduring individuals, and they formed the basis of the modern Trakehner.

The Trakehner today is one of the most beautiful and intelligent of the warmblood breeds, and it has played a role in the development of other breeds, including the Hanoverian.

Above Powerful, enduring and intelligent, the beautiful Trakehner stands at 15.2–17hh and can be any colour, with bay, grey, chestnut and black being the most common.

Opposite top This magnificent Trakehner stallion is surefooted enough to trot easily through the snow.

Opposite below The Trakehner's elegant and refined head is often finely chiselled and narrow at the muzzle, with a broad forehead.

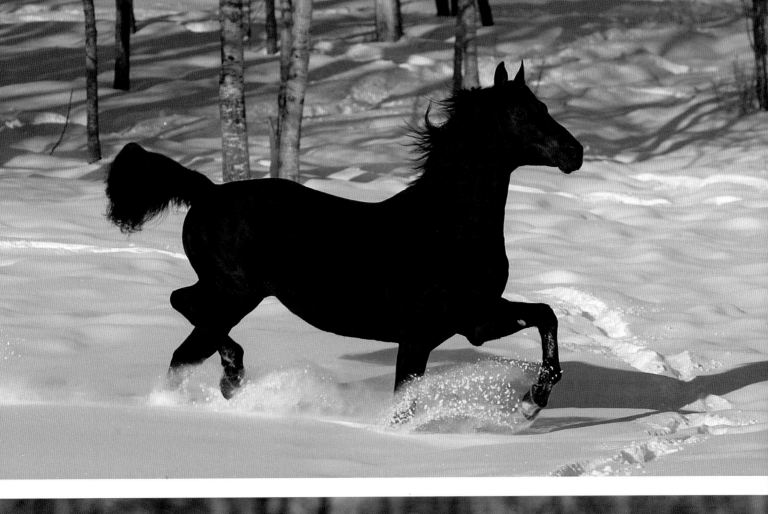
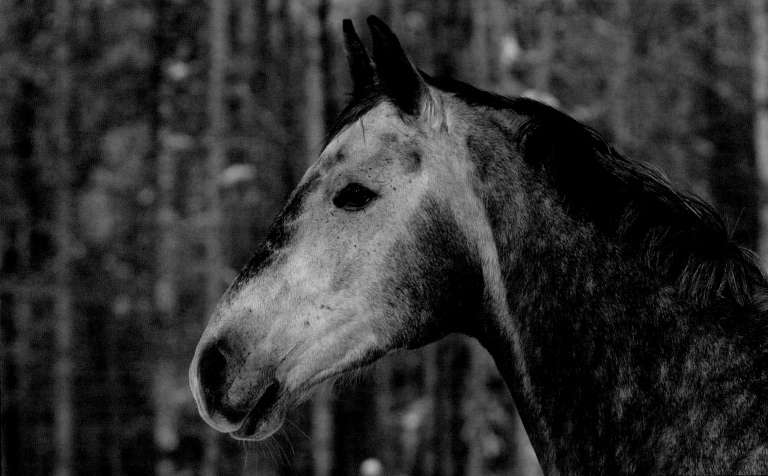

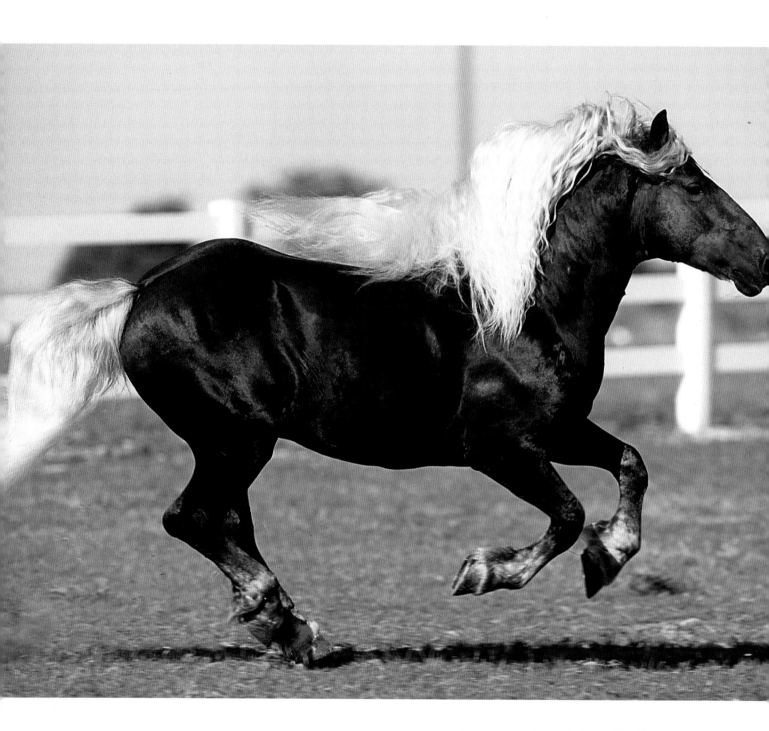

Above It is easy to see why this striking little horse is sometimes referred to as the 'pearl of the Black Forest'.

Black Forest Chestnut

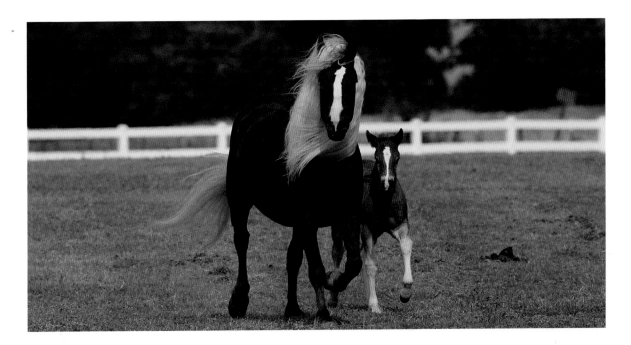

Known in its native country of Germany as the *Schwarzwalder Kaltblut*, or Black Forest Coldblood, this striking draught-type horse is comparatively rare. It is a small, hardy animal bred for working in forestry and on farmland. Farmers in the region called it the 'pearl of the Black Forest' due to its beauty and gentle disposition.

The breed dates back to around 600 years ago, and its first studbook was established at the end of the 19th century. State-regulated breeding stock ensured that only the best horses were bred from, and the Black Forest Chestnut was renowned for its high fertility, longevity and versatility. Attempts to increase the size of the breed using Belgian draught horses were resisted by private breeders, with the result that many foals were registered with forged papers and the breed remained pure.

As was the case with many of the working heavy horses, mechanization had an adverse effect on the breed and it became greatly endangered. By the 1980s there were only 160 registered broodmares. Today there are around 46 approved breeding stallions (with 16 at the state-owned stud in Marbach/Baden-Wurttemberg), and about 700 registered mares. The breed remains popular as a smart driving horse and a biddable riding horse.

Above A Black Forest Chestnut mare and her pretty foal, which will stand at around 15.2hh once mature.

Selle Français

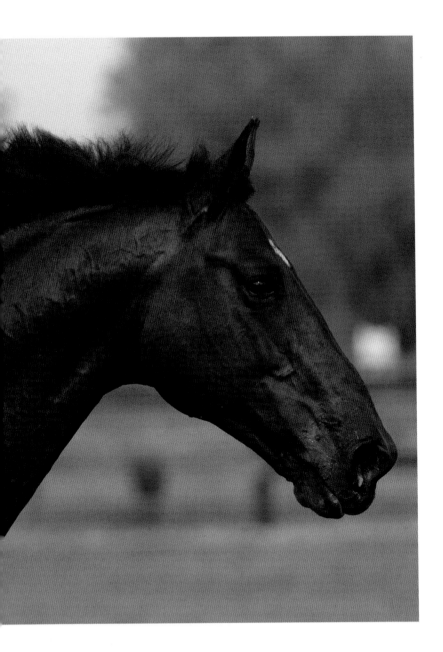

France's warmblood is a relatively new breed that was recognized in 1958 and had its first studbook published in 1965. Measuring at least 15hh and mainly chestnut in colour, the Selle Français was developed by crossing native stock with trotters, Thoroughbreds, Arabs and Anglo Arabs. All stock registered in the studbook has pedigrees tracing back generations, so that the breed is largely free from foreign blood.

The most dominant breed was the Anglo-Norman, developed in the 19th century by crossing Norfolk Trotters, Arabs and Thoroughbreds with the local heavyweight mares. An estimated 90 per cent of modern Selle Français contain Anglo-Norman blood. Charolais, Corlay, Anjou and Ardennes have also played a part in the development of the breed.

Thoroughbred stallions Furioso (perhaps the most influential sire in warmblood breeding), Rantzau and Ultimate can be found in virtually every successful modern Selle Français. While the breed occurs throughout France and is bred by both private and national studs, its 'spiritual home' is at the Saint-Lo national stud in Normandy. It has, however, earned its place as a world-class warmblood, competing with great success in most equestrian disciplines, particularly showjumping.

Left The Selle Français possesses the fine-boned, refined head that is typical of a warmblood breed.

Right This handsome young Selle Français is full of quality and should go on to excel in any discipline.

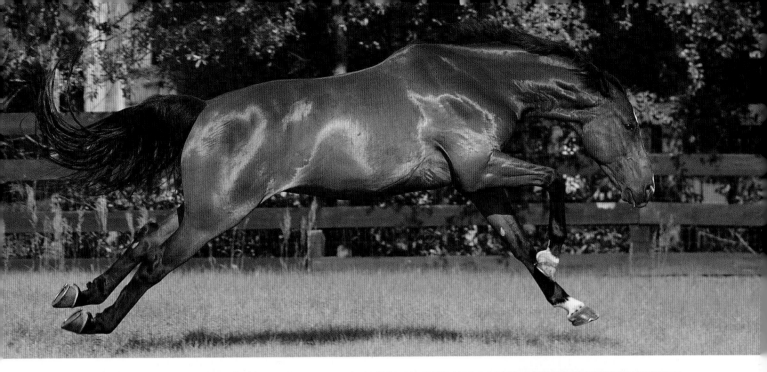

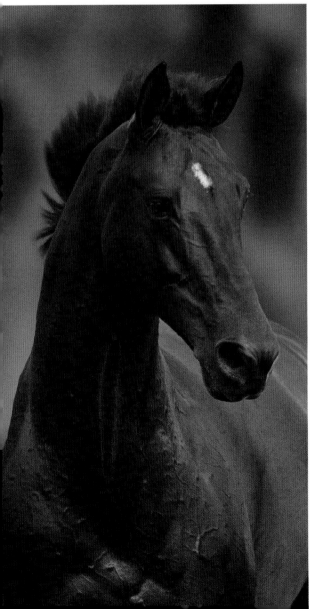

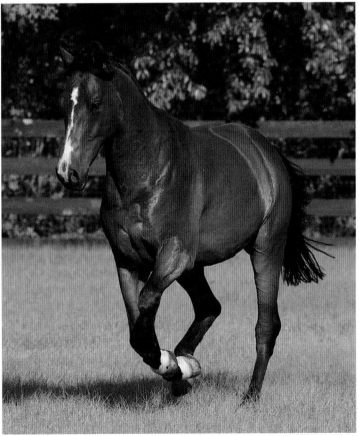

Top Full of joie de vivre, this Selle Français shows the power and speed of his ancestors.

Above A perfectly balanced collected canter shows off this Selle Français's sloping shoulder and sound limbs.

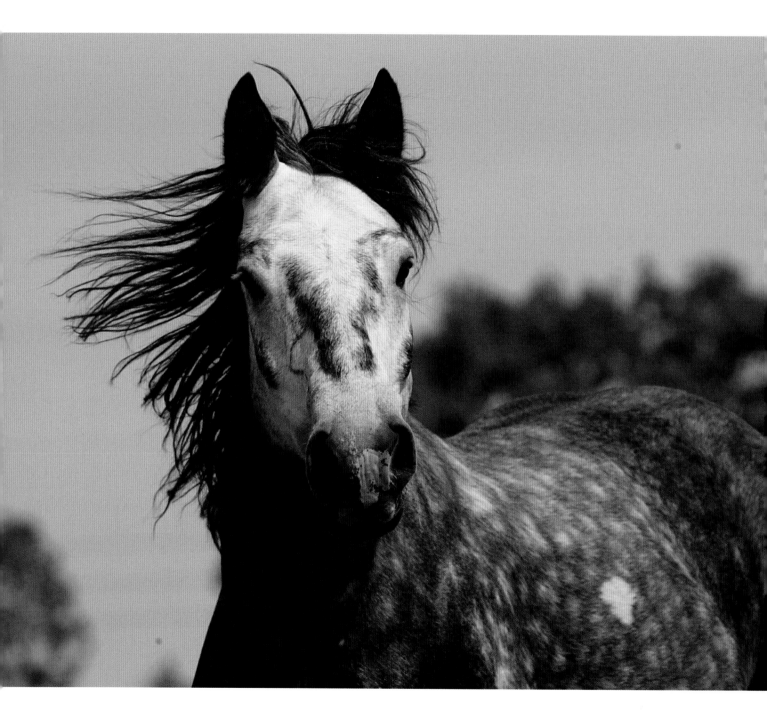

Above The Percheron has a surprisingly
refined head for a draught breed, no doubt
as a result of its Arab ancestry.

Percheron

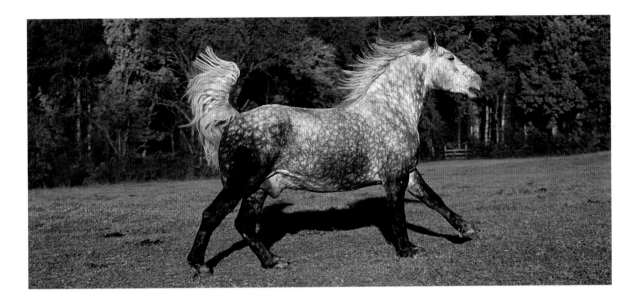

It is hard to believe that France's draught breed, the noble Percheron, is descended from Arab blood. It is thought that Arab horses abandoned by Moors fleeing after their defeat in the Battle of Poitiers in AD732 were crossed with the heavy Flemish stock in a district called La Perche, producing the Percheron. This handsome breed has therefore endured for 13 centuries.

Further Arab blood was added by the French government's stud at La Pin in a carefully selected breeding programme that used two Arab sires on chosen mares. The resulting animal was lighter than earlier Percherons, which were used primarily as warhorses and had to be able to carry armoured knights. The two important Arab sires were

Godolphin and Gallipoly, with the latter siring Jean Le Blanc. He was foaled in 1830 and is regarded as the founding stallion of the Percheron, to whom all modern Percherons trace their ancestry.

In the 18th century the Percheron was in demand as a coach horse. This was due to its good looks and power – a team of well-matched grey Percherons was a fine sight indeed. Because it was a strong and willing workhorse, it later became popular as an agricultural animal.

The modern Percheron stands at around 16hh and is predominantly grey – perhaps as evidence of its Arab heritage. It has a refined head and clean legs, with little feather for a draught breed, and is hard working and docile.

Above The dappled grey coat of this handsome Percheron perhaps derives from the Arab, which has played an important part in the breed's development.

Fjord

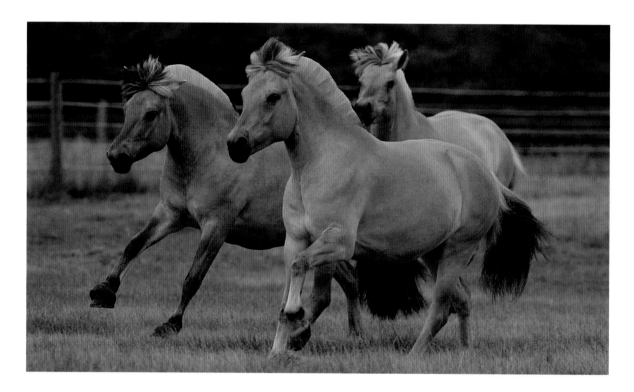

One of the world's oldest and purest breeds, Norway's Fjord, with its dun colouring, black points and stocky build, closely resembles Przewalski's Horse, although it has the usual 64 chromosomes of all equines rather than the 66 of Przewalski's Horse. It thus has more in common with the now-extinct Tarpan.

Little is known about the origins of the Fjord, but there have been wild horses in Sweden and Denmark since the Ice Age; it is thought that the Fjord originated there and made its way west. Viking burial grounds indicate that Fjord-type horses have been selectively bred by humans for some 2,000 years, and it appears that the Fjord is the descendant of the earliest horses in Norway.

There are two Fjord types in Norway: a relatively heavy, large horse with profuse hair and feathering, and a smaller, lighter type, which is in favour today. The most important stallion in the breed's history is Njål 166, who was born in 1891. He stood at stud from 1896 until his death in 1910, and can be traced in the pedigree of every living Norwegian Fjord.

Above Norway's Fjord is considered to be one of the world's oldest and purest horse breeds. It is stocky and muscular, with short, strong legs that have plenty of bone and good joints.

Opposite The upright, brushy mane of the Fjord is one of many features it shares with the primitive Przewalski's Horse. Its thick, shaggy coat protects it from the icy cold of the Norwegian winter.

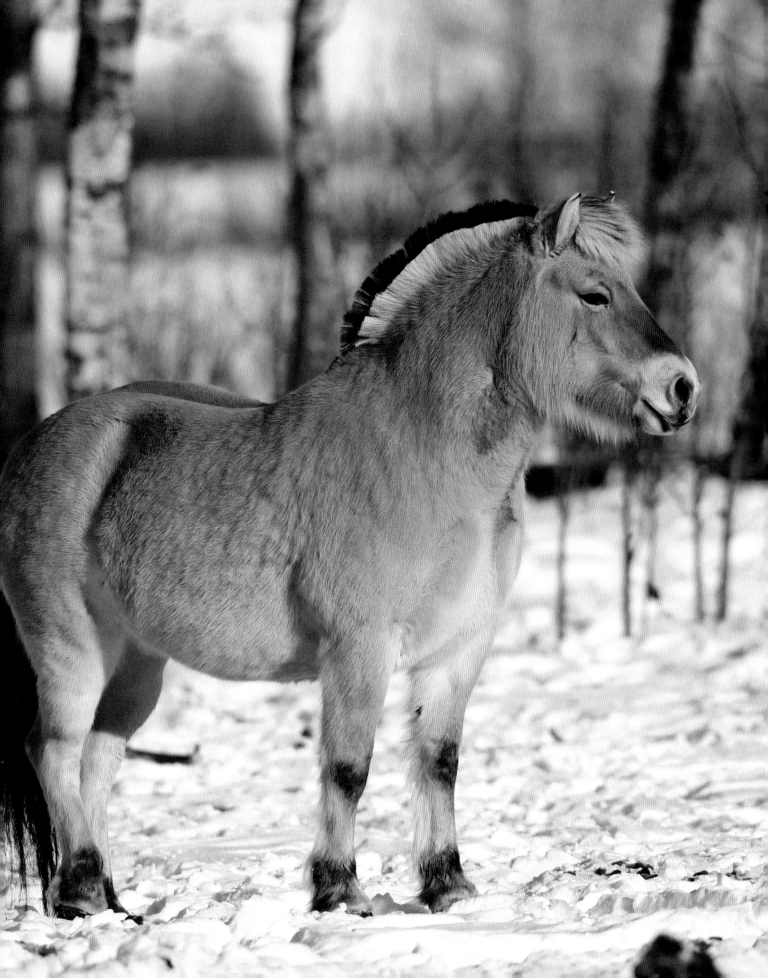

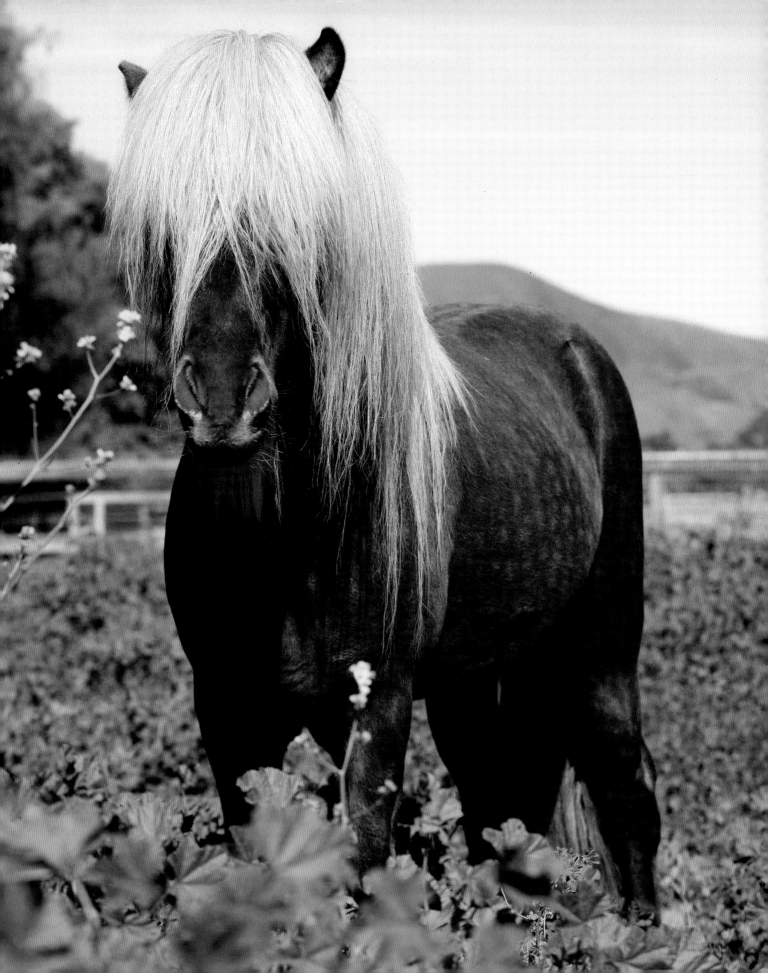

Icelandic

There is no word in Icelandic for 'pony', so Europe's northernmost country's native breed is always called a horse, despite its small stature. Iceland was first settled in the 9th century, and the first reference to the Icelandic horse occurs in the 12th century. Small and sturdy but not unattractive, the breed has evolved to cope well with the freezing temperatures of the 'land of fire and ice'. Many believe that a separate species of horse, *Equus scandianavicus*, once existed in Iceland and other Scandinavian countries, but that other European breeds were crossed with it and it was lost – except in Iceland, where it remained pure. Certainly, the Icelandic has a different genotype from that of other European horse populations.

In addition to the walk, trot, canter and gallop, the Icelandic horse possesses two other gaits – the *tölt*, a fast running walk similar to that found in American breeds, and the *skold*, a fast lateral gait used for running short distances. In the *skold*, horses can attain a speed of almost 30 miles an hour.

While the Icelandic has suffered losses over the years – it was almost wiped out in the 1700s due to volcanic eruptions – there are now an estimated 80,000 individuals in Iceland, and the breed is also popular as an export.

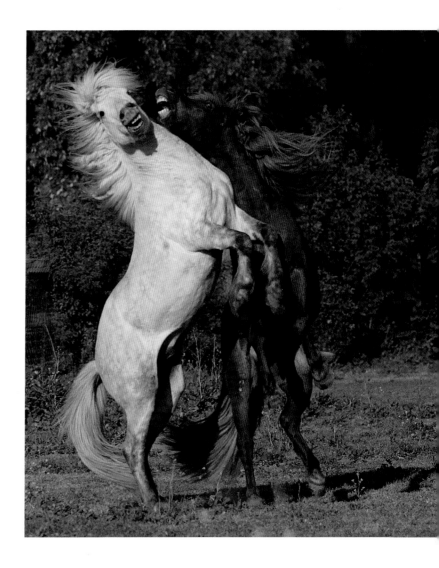

Opposite This enchanting Icelandic has a deep liver-chestnut coat with a flaxen mane and tail, but all colours are seen in the breed.

Above Two Icelandic stallions play fight – the breed is gentle and friendly, which makes it suitable for children as well as adults.

Lipizzaner

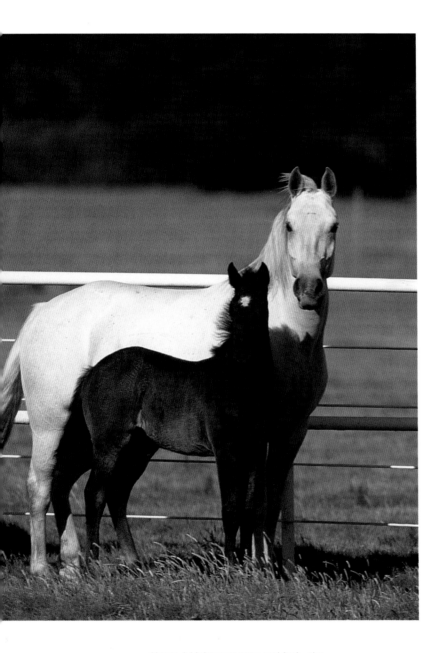

There are few sights more stirring than the dancing white stallions performing in the baroque splendour of the Spanish Riding School of Vienna. The horses were, however, originally bred for battle, not ballet. The Hapsburg family that controlled both Spain and Austria required light, fast horses for the military. In the late 16th century Emperor Maximillian II and his brother Archduke Charles both founded royal studs, the latter at Lipica, Trieste, near the Adriatic Sea in modern-day Slovenia. The stud was started with Spanish stock introduced during Moorish rule by crossing Barb and Arab stallions with Iberian mares; the result was a hardy, intelligent and beautiful horse. The breed was established using six main stallion lines: Conversano, born in 1767; Favory, 1779; Maestoso, 1819; Neapolitano, 1790; Pluto, 1765 and Siglavy, 1810.

During the First World War the breeding stock from Lipica was relocated to Laxenburg, near Vienna, while the foals were moved to the other imperial stud at Kladrub in the present-day Czech Republic. The breed came under threat of extinction during the Second World War, after the mares and foals were transferred to Hostau in Czechoslovakia by the Germans. It was saved from the advancing Soviet army through the heroic efforts of the Spanish Riding School's then director Alois Podhajsky, combined with strong American help. It is due to their efforts that the dancing white horses may be seen today in all their glory.

Above A Lipizzaner mare and foal – the youngsters are always born dark and turn grey as they get older.

Opposite This Lipizzaner stallion displays the spark and athleticism for which the breed is famed at the Spanish Riding School of Vienna.

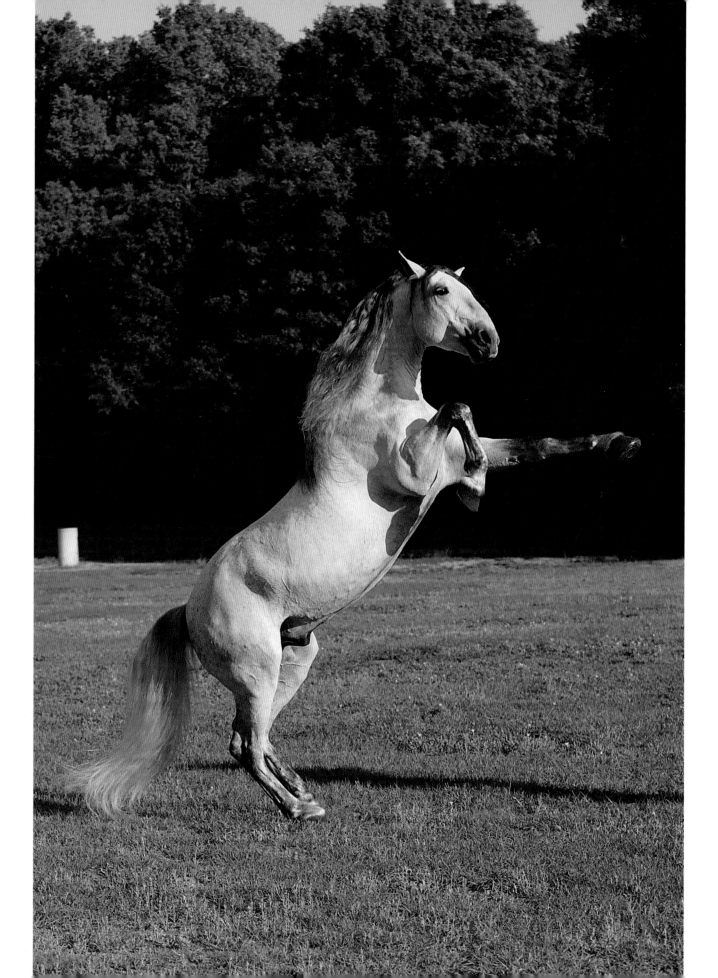

Belgian

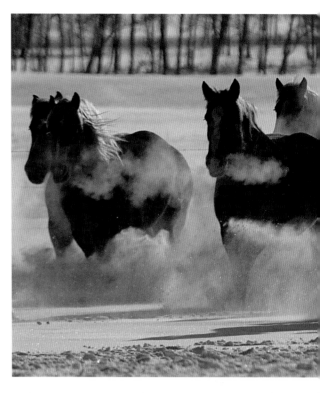

Belgium's heavy horse breed was developed in Brabant in the centre of the country – a fertile region that, together with good breeding practice, enabled the breed's success. Its foundation was the heavy black Flemish horse known to have been in Western Europe since at least the time of Julius Caesar, and to have carried armoured knights into war. The Belgian government played an energetic role in fixing the breed type by establishing a system of district shows throughout the country, culminating in the National Show in Brussels, an international showcase for the breed.

Belgian draught horses came to be regarded as a national treasure and were widely exported. In 1903 the Belgian government sent horses to the St Louis World Fair and the International Livestock Exposition in Chicago, and the United States embraced the breed with enthusiasm. All imports stopped with the onset of the First World War, but the United States had enough stock to continue to breed this popular little draught horse.

In its home country the breed suffered following the two world wars. Numbers dropped from some 200,000 individuals in Belgium in 1950, to fewer than 6,000 in 1980. However, the popularity of the sturdy and handsome Belgian has recovered, and it is regularly used today as a show, driving and riding horse.

Right The sturdy Belgian breed, which stands at around 17hh, is attractive for a draught breed, with a refined head.

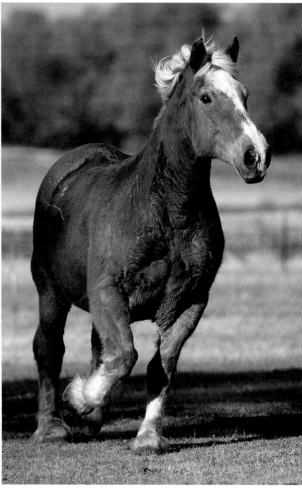

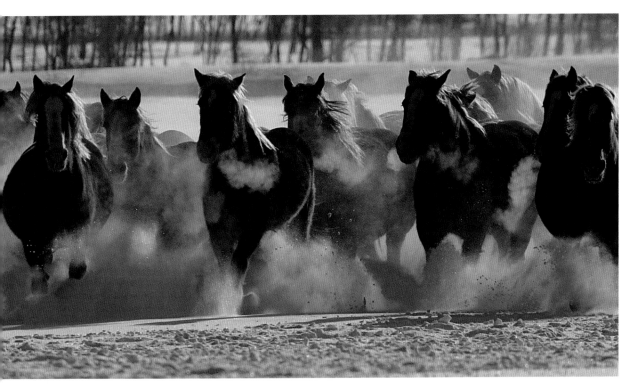

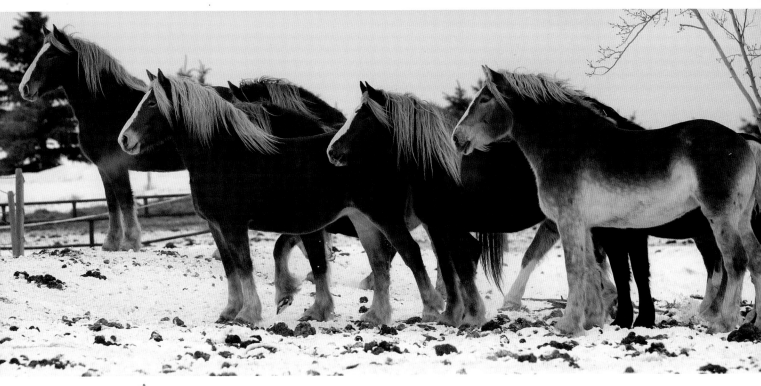

Top Belgian horses in the snow in Canada
– the breed is widely exported and popular in
North America.

Above The Belgian is usually light chestnut
in colour, with a flaxen mane and tail.

Haflinger

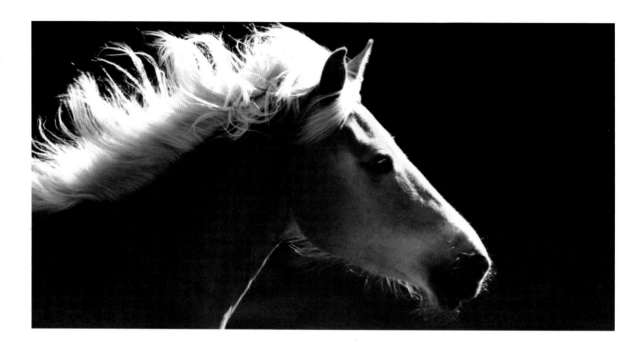

Bright as a copper coin, Austria's Haflinger is named after the Tyrolean village of Hafling, where this breed originated. It is thought that native ponies, a coarse breed used on the mountain farms, were crossed with Arabs to produce the breed. Its foundation sire is widely recognized to have been 249 Folie, who was foaled in 1874. All modern Haflingers can trace back to Folie through seven bloodlines. The Haflinger suffered as a result of the two world wars, when poorer quality stallions were used to save it from extinction, resulting in a heavier, draught-type animal. After 1946 breeders focused on producing finer, pure-bred Haflingers, and created a closed studbook. By 2005 there were an estimated 250,000 Haflingers worldwide. In 2003 a Haflinger became the first horse to be cloned, the result being a filly called Prometea.

The Haflinger is an attractive, active little creature ranging from light palomino to rich chestnut set off by a flaxen mane and tail. Although it stands at only 14.3hh, it is considered to be more of a horse than a pony and is tough and agile. Reared on the mountain slopes, the Haflinger is surefooted and long-lived, with a lifespan of up to 40 years. It is suitable as a riding pony both for adults due to its strength and for children because of its calm nature.

Above The Haflinger has a pretty, pony-type head that is lean and refined, and a large and expressive eye.

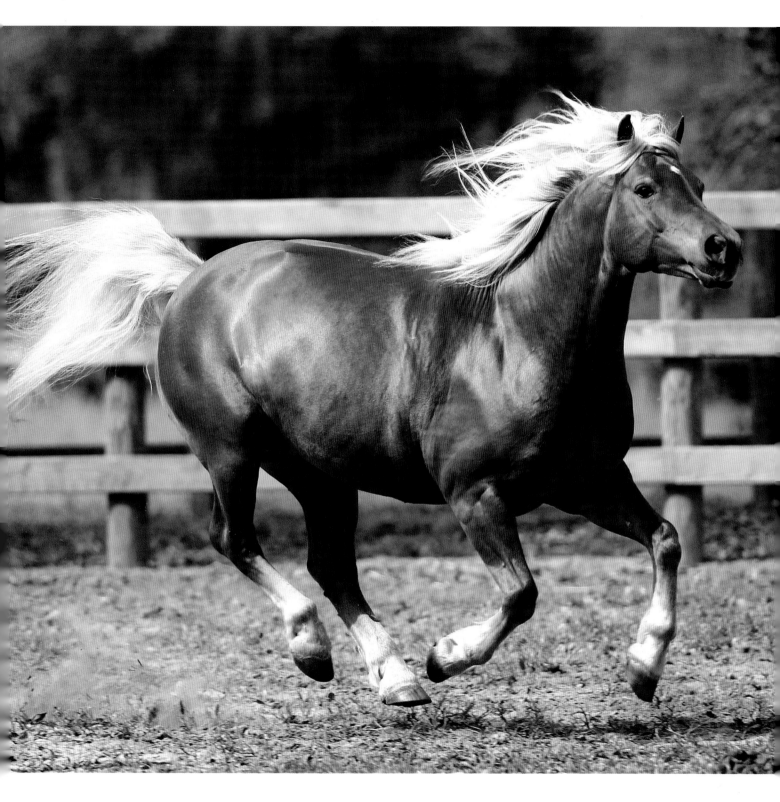

Above The striking Haflinger is surefooted and hardy, accustomed to working the mountain slopes of its native Austria.

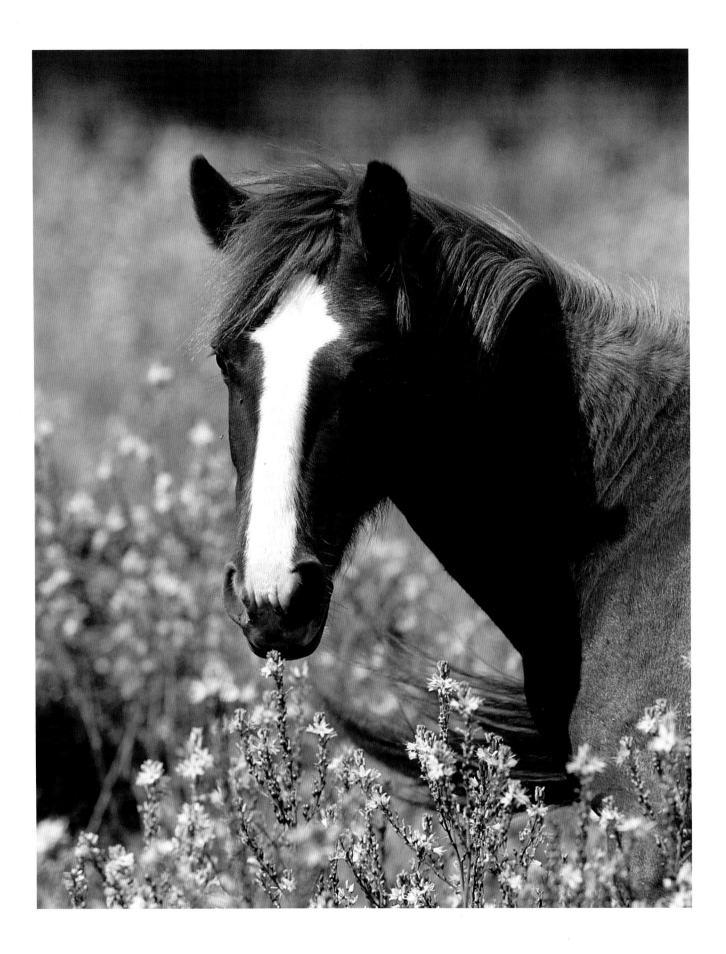

Giara

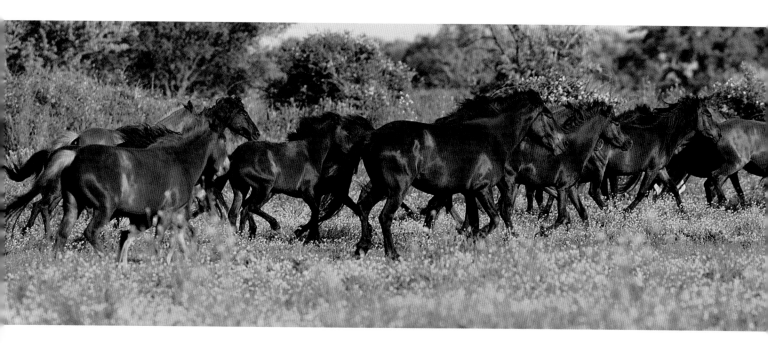

Mystery surrounds the origins of the Giara, Sardinia's only native breed. Fossil finds suggest that it dates back to the late Iron Age, around AD500, and may have been introduced to the island by Phoenician or Greek navigators in 500–400BC. The breed takes its name from the Giara di Gesturi, a high, steep plateau in southern Sardinia. At one time there were large herds of Giara in the highlands, on the tip of Capo Caccia and within the state forest of Porto Conte.

The result of volcanic activity, with cooling lava floes forming a protective barrier for the underlying rock, the Giara di Gesturi rises some 1,640 feet above the surrounding countryside. It was a harsh and unforgiving home to these little equines, and its isolated location resulted in the breed being left largely untouched for centuries.

Only a few hundred Giara remain on the uncontaminated oasis of the plateau. Still running wild in small family herds, they are now owned by the XXV Comunita Montana Sa Giara, through funding by the Sardinian government. Within a government programme, they have been crossed with Arab, Anglo Arab and German riding ponies to create the Giarab, a new breed that is suited for equestrian sports.

Opposite Sardinia's only equine breed stands at barely more than 13.1hh, though it is definitely regarded as a horse rather than a pony. It has a rather large head with a wide jaw, set on a short, strong neck.

Above Living on the isolated Giara di Gesturi in southern Sardinia, the agile, surefooted Giara is very well suited to its rocky mountainous homeland.

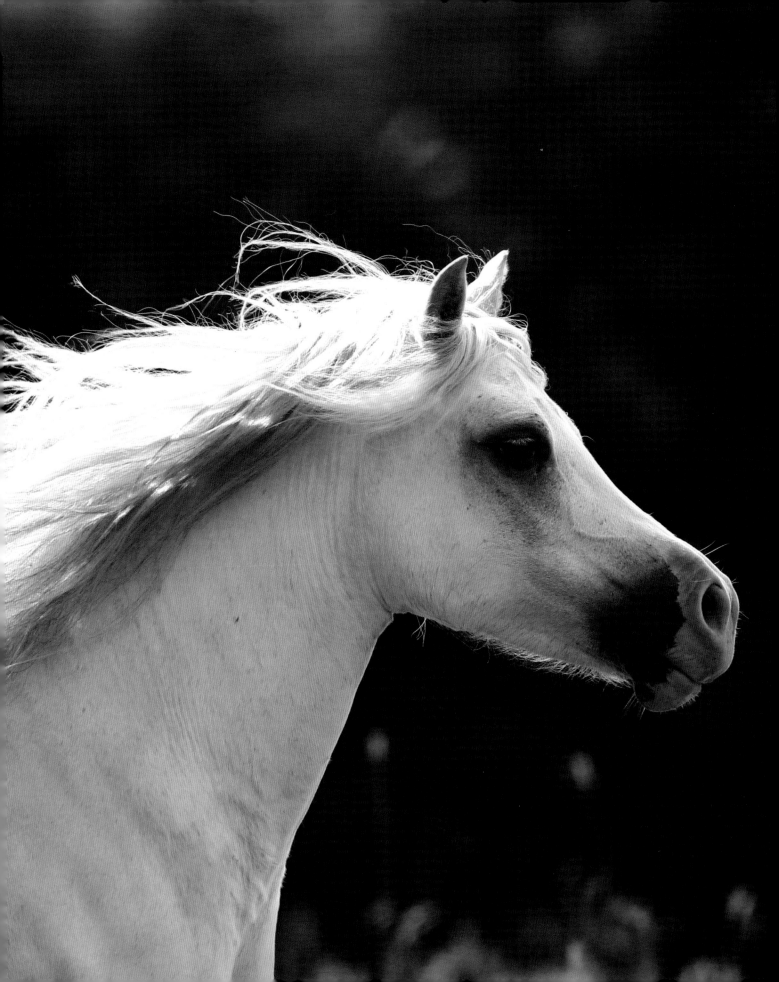

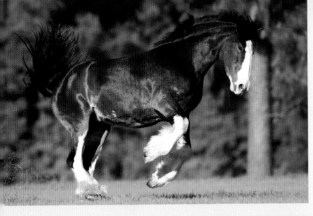

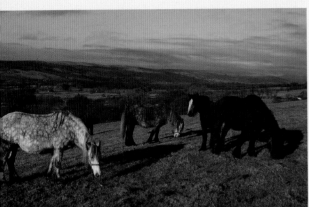

United Kingdom

Britain's comparative isolation led to her equines remaining relatively pure. This was particularly the case with breeds like the Exmoor, which inhabited the wild moors of south-west England, and the Welsh Mountain Pony. However, Britain's invasions and excursions also resulted in the introduction of a number of new bloodlines.

Clockwise from far left Welsh Section A (page 102); Shire (page 85); Dales (page 98); Highland (page 90).

Suffolk

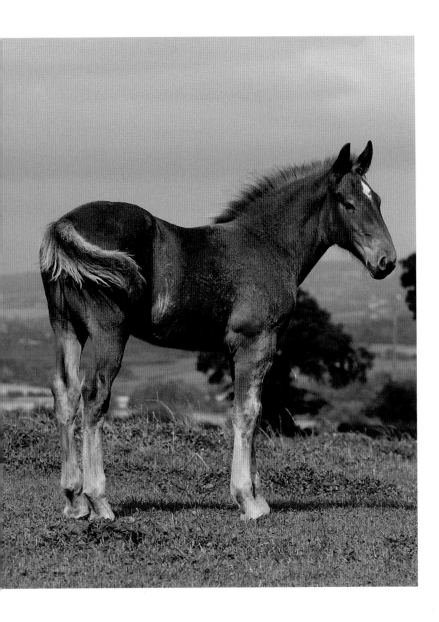

The stocky, four-square appearance of East Anglia's heavy horse earned it the moniker Suffolk Punch, while its rich colour resulted in the title Suffolk Sorrel. More correctly, however, it is simply the Suffolk, and it is thought to be Britain's oldest heavy horse. All Suffolks alive today can trace their male line back to one stallion, Crisp's Horse of Ufford, foaled in 1768.

The Suffolk is always chestnut – spelled without the middle 't' in the case of this breed – ranging from light golden through liver to deep red. American author Marguerite Henry, best known for her novel *Misty of Chincoteague*, wrote of the Suffolk: 'His colour is bright chestnut, like a tongue of fire against black field furrows, against green corn blades, against yellow wheat, against blue horizons. Never is he any other colour.'

The Suffolk is massively built, but has a lot of quality. Unlike other draught breeds it does not have much feather on its strong legs; this would have been a disadvantage when working the heavy clay soil for which its home county is known. Suffolk and its neighbour Norfolk are bordered to the north, east and south by the North Sea, so the Suffolk horse, bred for power, stamina and longevity, has been kept remarkably pure. Although it is still popular for its intelligence and beauty, it is listed as 'critical' by the Rare Breeds Survival Trust.

Above This Suffolk foal already has the four-square, butty appearance of the breed, which gave it the name 'Suffolk Punch'.

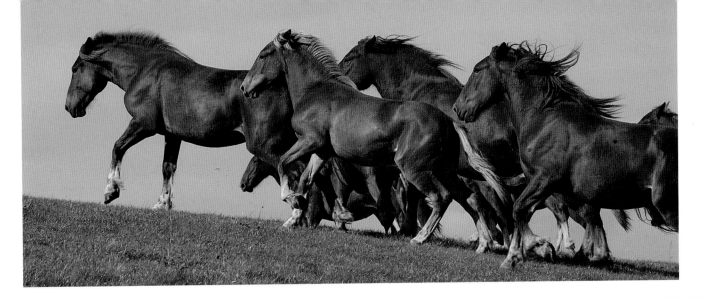

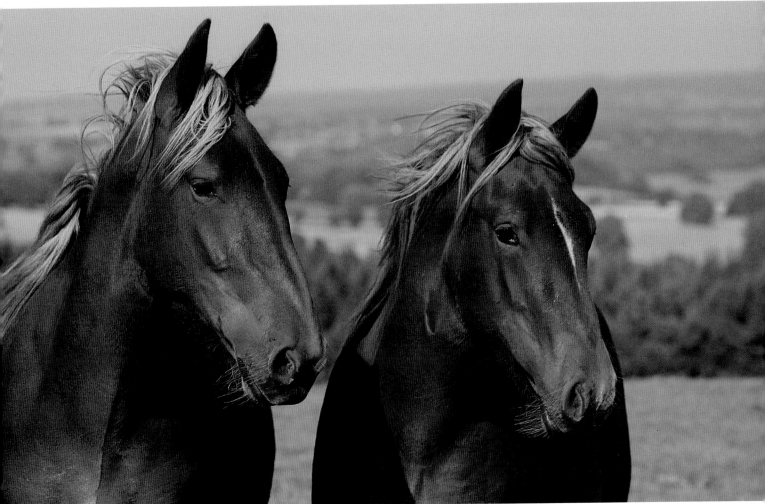

Top The Suffolk is always coloured chesnut
– correctly spelled without the middle 'T'.

Above These Suffolk horses show the
elegance and quality typical of the breed,
despite its powerful frame.

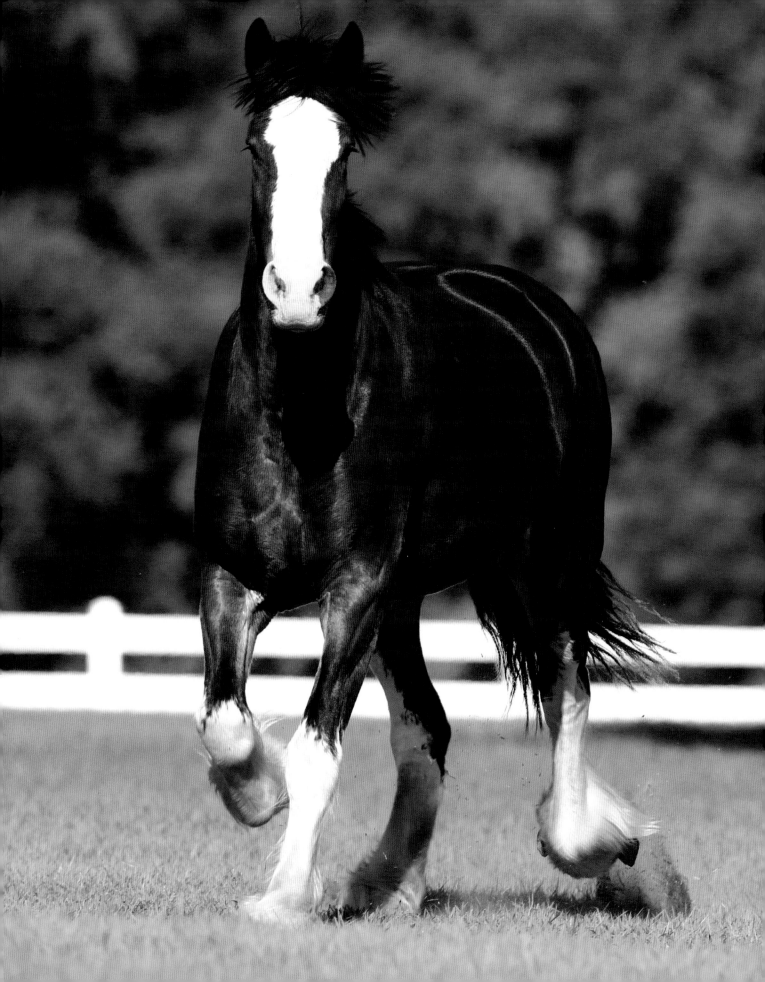

Shire

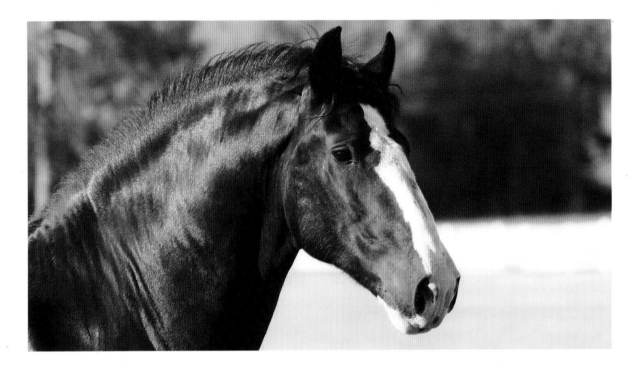

The word 'shire', after which this breed is named, is thought to come from the old Saxon word *schyran*, meaning to divide or shear, and it was used to define many of what are now England's counties. It is known that huge horses existed in Britain for thousands of years – the English Great Horse was chronicled by the Romans, who landed in the country in the 1st century AD. The Shire was developed over the ages from a mighty animal bred for war, capable of carrying a knight in full armour. A gentle giant, it was known by many names in the course of its development: the Great Horse, the War Horse, the Old English Black and the Lincolnshire Giant. However, it was King Henry VIII who is credited with applying the name 'Shire' to the breed.

The Shire was influenced by blood from Flemish horses imported in the 1100s and was a typical 'coldblood', as dull in colour as it was in personality. At this time it was known as the Old English Black. In the 1800s a breeder called Robert Bakewell endeavoured to improve it. For some years it was known as the Bakewell Black, but the latter part of its name became a misnomer as the outside blood resulted in a whole spectrum of coat colours.

Opposite The Shire is one of the world's biggest horse breeds, usually standing at around 17.3hh, although some individuals grow to more than 20hh.

Above The Shire has a long, lean profile that is sometimes slightly convex, small ears for a heavy breed and a kind eye.

Clydesdale

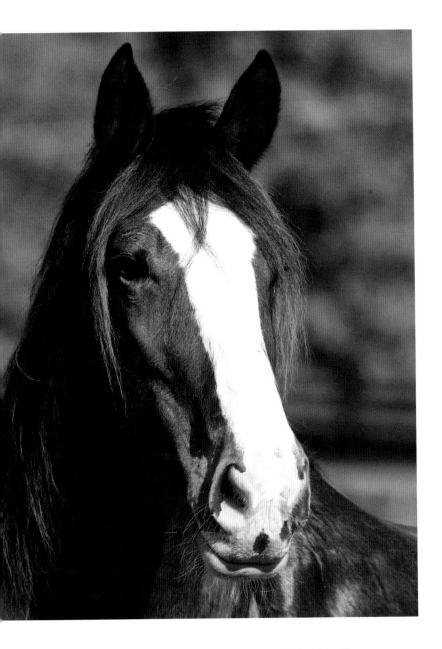

A Flemish stallion added size and substance to the native horses of Lanarkshire, in Scotland – a region that used to be known as Clydesdale. The stallion was imported in the mid-18th century by the Sixth Duke of Hamilton, who made him available free of charge to his tenants for use on their mares. Another Flemish stallion was brought to Scotland from England by John Paterson of Lochlyloch, and Lochlyloch blood became highly sought after. The goal of the farmers of Scotland was to produce a strong, powerful horse with quality. A black colt foal, known as 'Thompson's Black Horse', or Glancer, is thought to have been the first of the new breed to have its pedigree recorded, and he can be found in the lineage of all Clydesdales today. The breed society was established in 1877.

At one time there were an estimated 140,000 working horses in Scotland, plus many more in towns and cities; most were probably Clydesdales. The breed's popularity and versatility were such that in 1911, 1,617 stallions were exported. Three years later Clydesdales were conscripted by the army to serve in the First World War.

While the horses continued to be exported – in the period between 1850 and 1945 more than 20,000 Clydesdales were shipped to North and South America, Russia, Italy and Austria – the breed went into decline in its native Scotland as the tractor took over from traditional horsepower. Although numbers have improved, the Clydesdale remains endangered.

Above The Clydesdale shares similarities with the Shire, but has a straighter profile.

Right This Clydesdale mare and foal both have the characteristic white face of the breed.

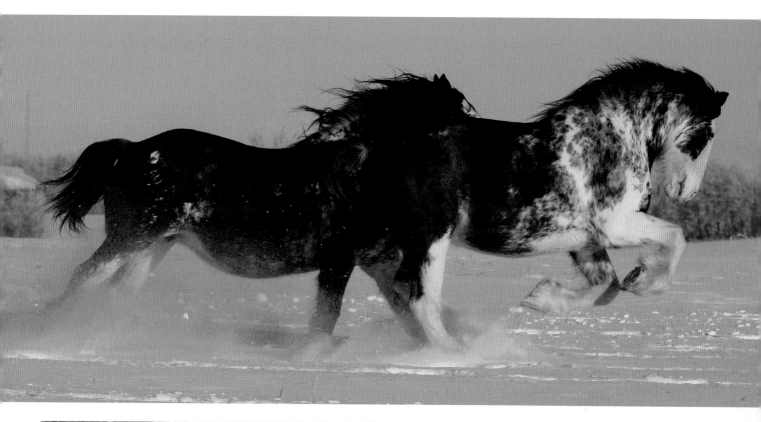

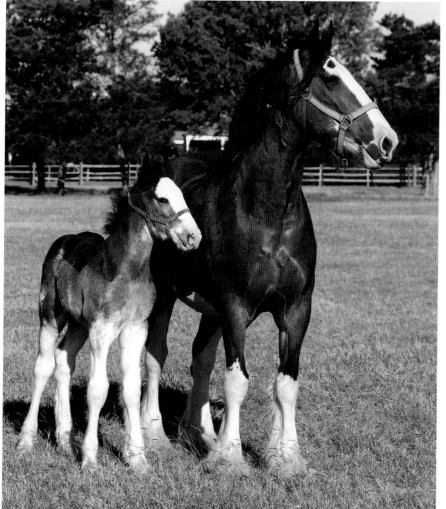

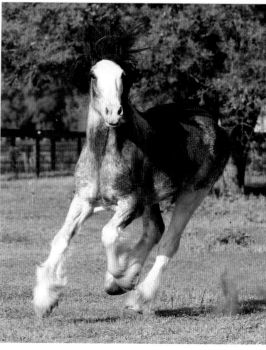

Top The Clydesdale is powerful and amazingly agile for a draught horse, with long legs and sound feet.

Above A considerable amount of white on the body and legs is a feature of the Clydesdale, as can be seen in this charming foal.

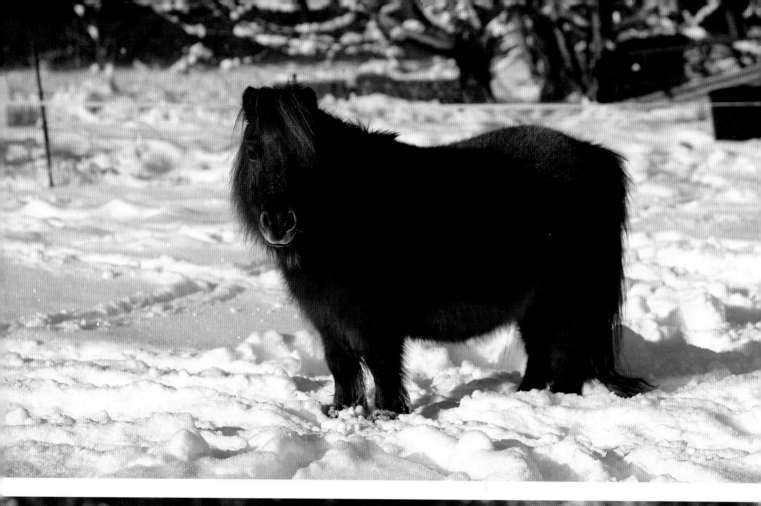
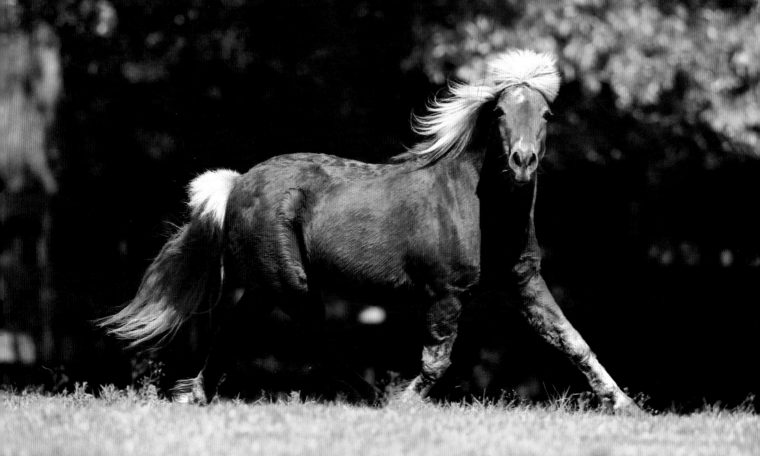

Shetland

There is evidence of tiny ponies living on the Shetland Isles, off the north coast of Scotland, since the Bronze Age. The islands were practically barren, with an unforgiving climate. With a thick coat, long mane and forelock, and short stature that protect it from the howling winds, the Shetland pony has adapted to survive all weathers in the open.

The islanders domesticated their indigenous equines, and the ponies were used to carry seaweed from the shore for use as a fertilizer, as well as peat from the bogs to burn as fuel. Under these tough conditions, nothing went to waste. It is indicative of the high regard in which the islanders held their tough little ponies that one of the earliest laws to be passed dictated 'cut any other man's horse-tail or main [*sic*] under the pain of ten pounds'.

The pony carries on its broad back the history of the Shetland Isles – and their fortunes. As well as being used to haul peat and seaweed, it was made to pull the cart and plough the land, then put into the coalmines of mainland Britain as a pit pony. Its strength and endurance made it ideal for this task, and Shetlands were also exported to work in the coalmines of the eastern United States, where the last pony mine closed in 1971. The mines went, but the Shetland remains popular as a riding pony for adults and children alike.

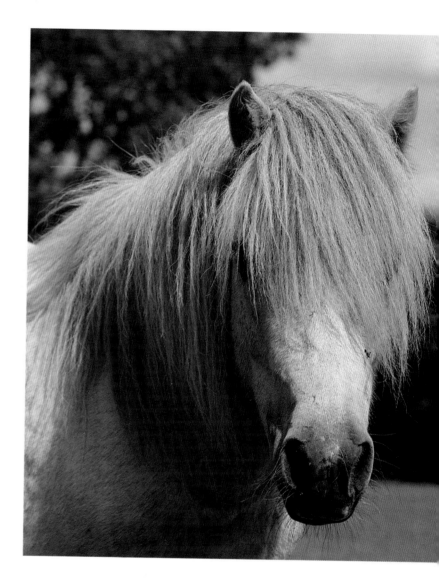

Opposite top The Shetland's thick coat and long mane and tail protect it from the elements.

Opposite below The Shetland has a well-defined wither, sloping shoulder, broad quarters and strong legs, making it quick and agile. It can be stubborn and wilful, but has a considerable amount of character.

Above All colours can be seen in the Shetland, including broken-coated as well as black, grey and chestnut.

Highland

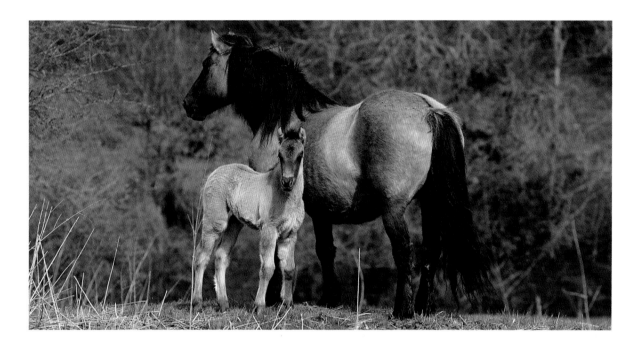

One of the largest and most versatile of Britain's native ponies, the Highland comes from the islands and highlands of Scotland. It is suggested that these animals were among the fauna that spread into Scotland with the retreat of the mighty glaciers of the last Ice Age, more than 10,000 years ago. However, it is equally likely that equines were brought to Scotland by the first settlers in prehistoric times. Certainly, there were horses in the country by at least 8BC, and they were used in Pictish times in around AD550–800.

The Highland pony has proven pedigrees that date back to the 1880s. It was used as a universal workhorse throughout Scotland, right up to the borders. Because of the country's inaccessibility several sub-types came into being, including Islay, Rhum, Mull and Barra strains. In 1890 the Department of Agriculture for Scotland founded the Faillie Stud, the objective of which was to improve the Highland pony.

The Highland was strong, sturdy, hard working and gentle to handle. Queen Victoria began a long association of the royal family with the breed, which continues today. The current British queen breeds ponies under her Balmoral prefix – these shine in the showring, both in-hand and under saddle.

Above This Highland mare with her charming dun-coloured foal has the 'primitive' dorsal stripe down her back.

Opposite Standing at around 14.2hh, the Highland is one of the biggest of Britain's native breeds.

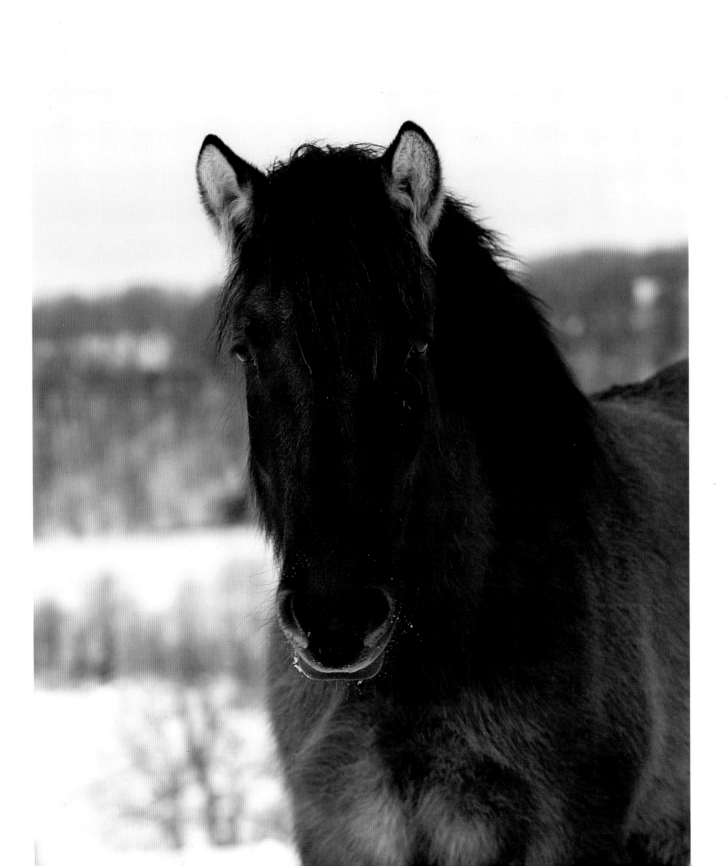

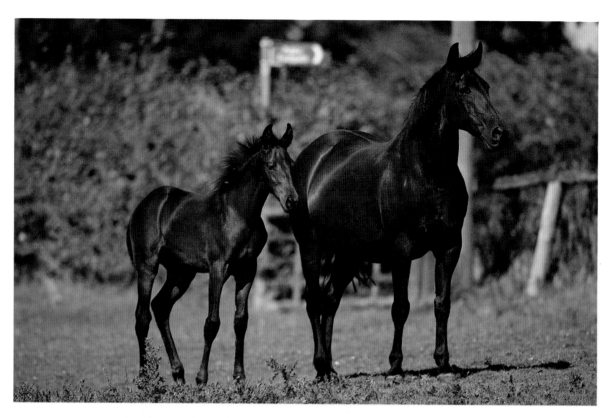

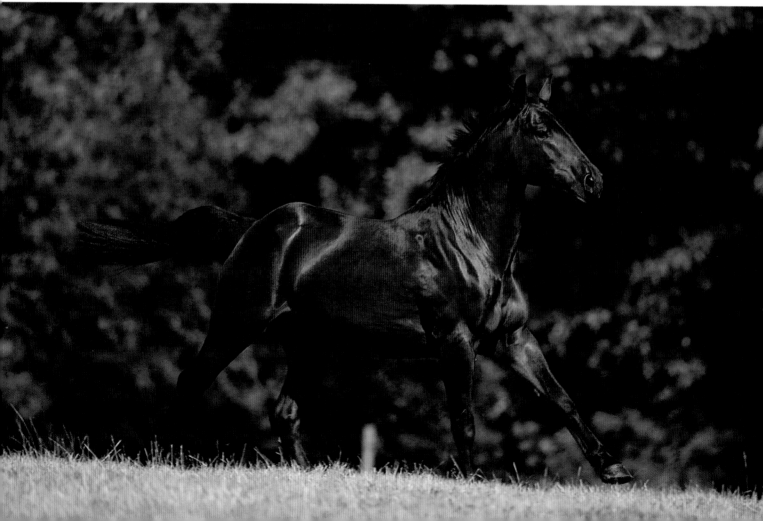

Cleveland Bay

Thought to be the oldest of all the British breeds, the Cleveland Bay takes its name from its colouring and from the Cleveland district of Yorkshire. In the 17th century native mares, which were rather dull and plain, were bred to Oriental stallions imported to Britain. The result of this was a quality horse of uniform colour standing at 16–16.2hh, and possessing substance and longevity.

As well as being used as coach and hunt horses, Cleveland Bays were used as pack horses by the chapmen – the travelling salesmen of the day – and for some time they were known as Chapman horses. As Britain's roads improved people wanted and expected faster journey times. Thoroughbred blood, which had been developed shortly before with the arrival of Arab and Barb horses, was used to give the Cleveland Bay more pace. The coaching era was short-lived, and as the railways developed the Cleveland Bay fell out of favour; by the 1880s it was teetering on the brink of extinction. The Cleveland Bay Society was established in 1884 to preserve and promote the breed.

The Queen was to give the breed a boost, buying a pure-bred Cleveland Bay colt called Mulgrave Supreme in 1961 and making him available at public stud. Today the Cleveland Bay is still used in royal ceremonial duties.

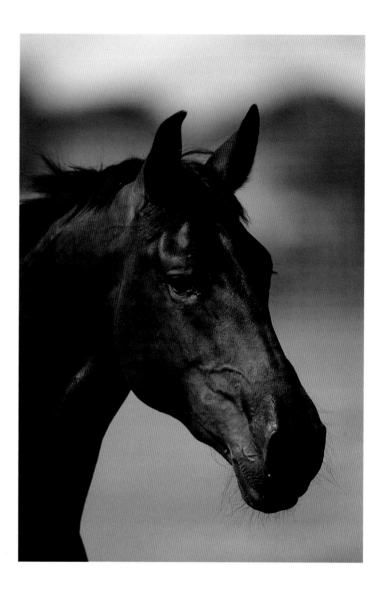

Opposite top This foal is a perfect match for its dam; the breed is always bay.

Opposite below A Cleveland Bay stallion shows off the paces that made the breed so popular for carriage driving.

Above The Cleveland Bay has a fine head, long, lean neck and sloping shoulder.

New Forest

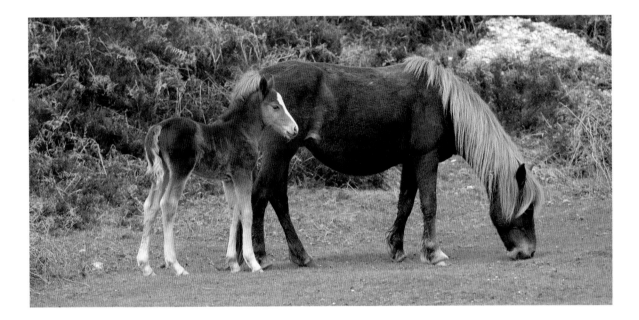

Perhaps the least known of Britain's native breeds, the elegant ponies that roam the New Forest in southern England have existed for centuries. Over time the blood of Welsh, Arab, Thoroughbred, Hackney and other native breeds was introduced to the New Forest pony to improve it. Relatively recently, perhaps to give the breed more substance and reinforce its 'pony' traits, Fell, Dales, Highland, Dartmoor and Exmoor bloodlines were introduced.

The New Forest remains one of largest areas of unenclosed land in Britain and was once a royal hunting ground. In 1016 rights of common pasture were granted to the people living in the forest.

The ponies in the forest are not feral. They are managed and looked after by the Commoners, their owners, and the Agisters, who are employed by the New Forest Verderers, an ancient body charged with running the New Forest alongside the Forestry Commission.

New Forest ponies form family groups, usually a mare, her daughters and their foals – stallions do not run free in the forest. Each autumn all the ponies are rounded up in what are known as 'drifts'. The animals are removed from the forest, the foals are branded and all the ponies are checked for health and wormed. There are currently around 4,500 ponies in the New Forest.

Above A mare and her foal graze peacefully in the New Forest, which gave the breed its name.

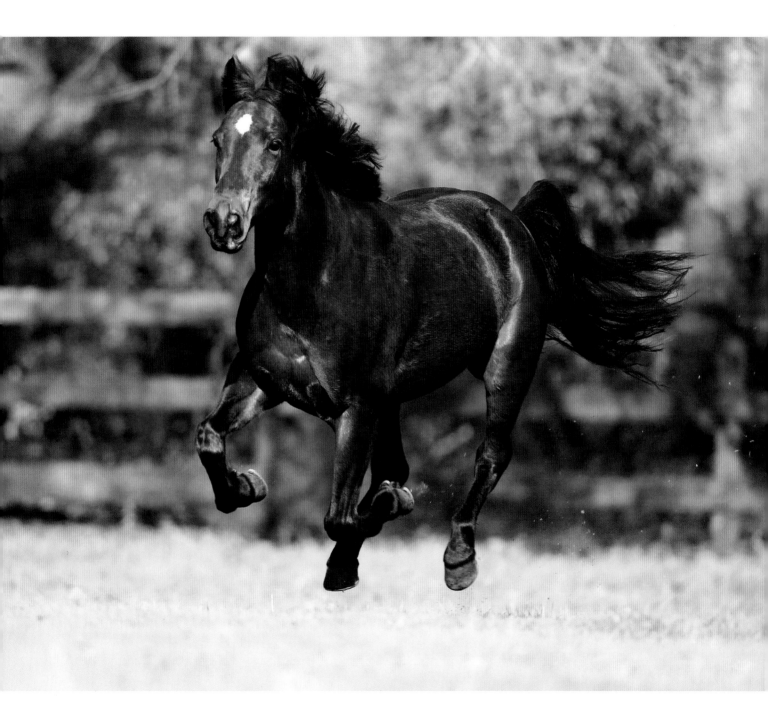

Above The New Forest pony stands at 14.2hh.
Both Arab and Thoroughbred blood have been
used to refine it and give it additional speed.

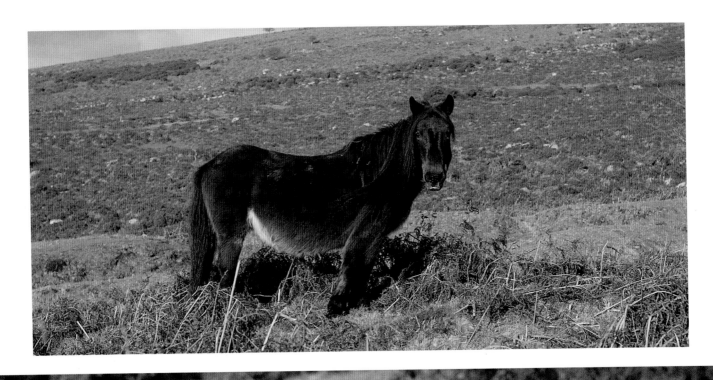

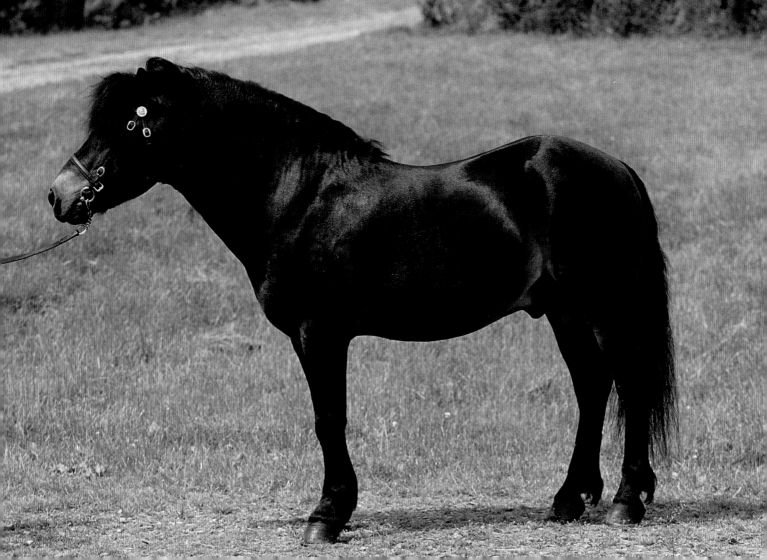

Dartmoor

In 1012 a Dartmoor pony was mentioned in the will of the Saxon bishop Aelfwold of Crediton. This is the earliest known reference to the tough little equines of the moors of south-west England. Although they stood at little more than 13hh, these ponies were extremely hardy and agile. They were used for centuries to work the tin mines, but their small stature made them unsuitable as warhorses. In 1535 King Henry VIII made it an offence to breed small equines. While many horse owners did strive to breed larger horses, this legislation was undoubtedly ignored in the remote areas of Dartmoor, as the little ponies were valued by the landowners.

In the 18th century small horses were in demand again for working in the coalmines and also for the game of polo, brought back from India (page 11), for which the agile Dartmoor was highly suited. In 1893 the Polo Pony Society – now the National Pony Society – was formed. In 1899 a section of the studbook was opened for 'mountain and moorland' ponies. Five stallions and 72 mares were entered into the first studbook. Among ponies later registered in the studbook were those owned by the director of Her Majesty's Prison at Princeton, Dartmoor, whose warders rode them when escorting convicts for their work outside the prison. Warders continued to ride Dartmoors to escort prisoners up until the 1960s. The breed suffered declines after the two world wars and is comparatively rare today, with an estimated total of 7,000 pure-bred Dartmoors in existence.

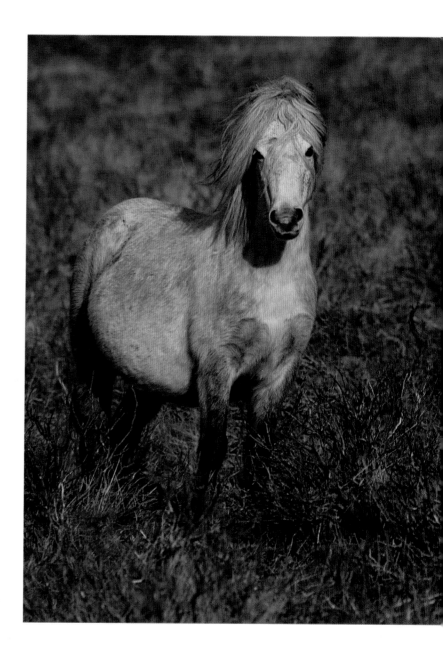

Opposite top A Dartmoor pony in the wide-open spaces of the moor in south-west England from which it takes its name.

Opposite below The Dartmoor stands at around 12.2hh and is compact and well made.

Above Most colours can be found in the Dartmoor, including roan, although never piebald or skewbald.

Dales

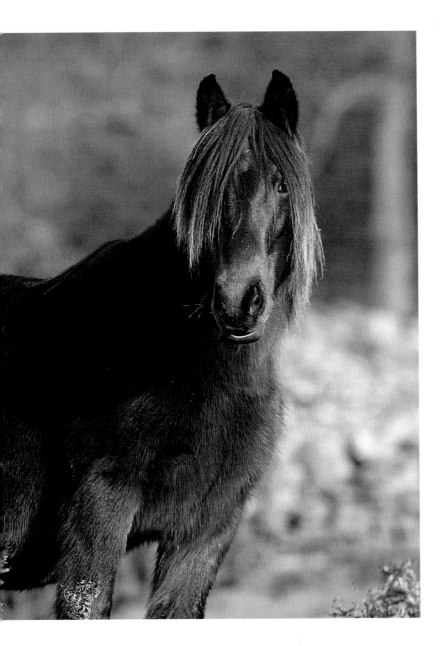

Lead mining constituted big business in northern England from Roman times, spreading from the eastern slopes of the mighty Pennine Range in Derbyshire to the Cheviot Hills close to the Scottish border. The lead had to be transported from the hills to the north-east coast, and was carried by teams of 9–10 sturdy pack ponies overseen by one mounted man. The breed used was the now-extinct, tough but plain Scottish Galloway, which was allowed to run with native mares near the mines. The Dales pony is the result of this custom. Hardy and agile, the Dales was renowned for its iron constitution, strength and endurance. It could carry two 'pigs' of lead weighing around two hundredweight, and travel up to a hundred miles a week over testing terrain.

As lead mining declined, farmers of the Dales uplands in turn discovered the value of the ponies. They could pull the plough or cart and cover considerable distances at speed, and were agile enough to shepherd sheep and clever enough jumpers to be able to do a day's hunting.

When trotting races became popular, the farmers – unable to afford to keep both a Dales pony and a trotter – used trotter blood on their ponies. The Dales was further boosted in the early 20th century when a British army captain acting for the Ministry of Agriculture stated that: 'Your breed has one superb asset, possessed of every specimen I saw, the most perfect foot in the British Isles.' Today the Dales is still renowned for its active, athletic trot.

Above The Dales has a neat, pony-like head with a straight profile, strong neck and long, sloping shoulder.

Opposite Standing at around 14.2hh, the Dales makes a good riding or driving pony and is powerful enough to carry an adult.

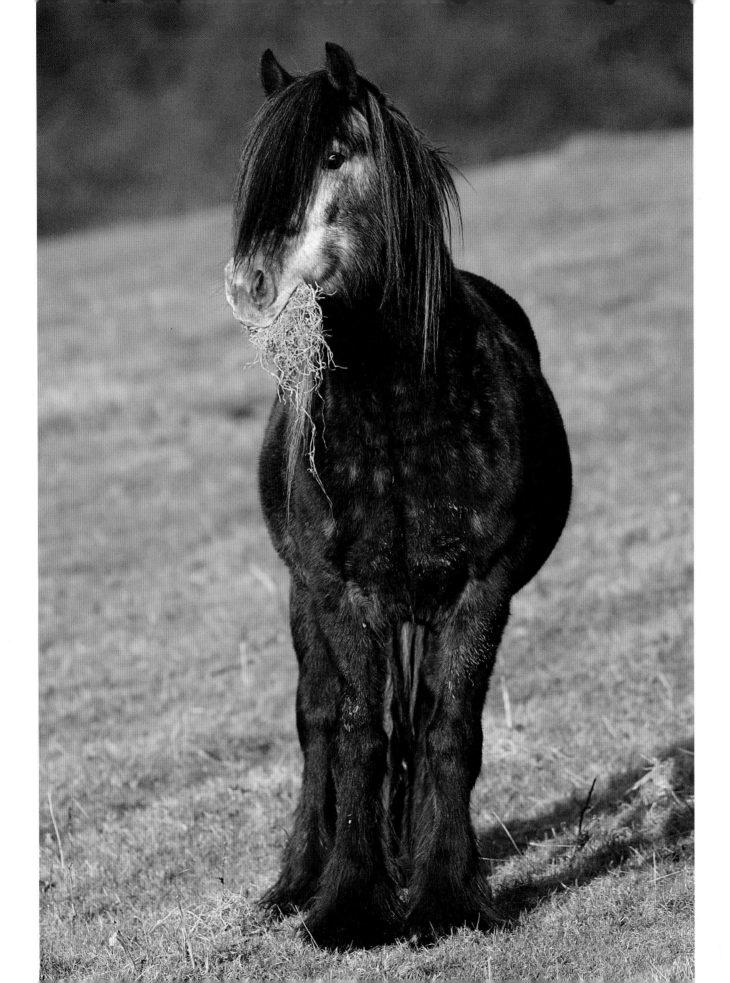

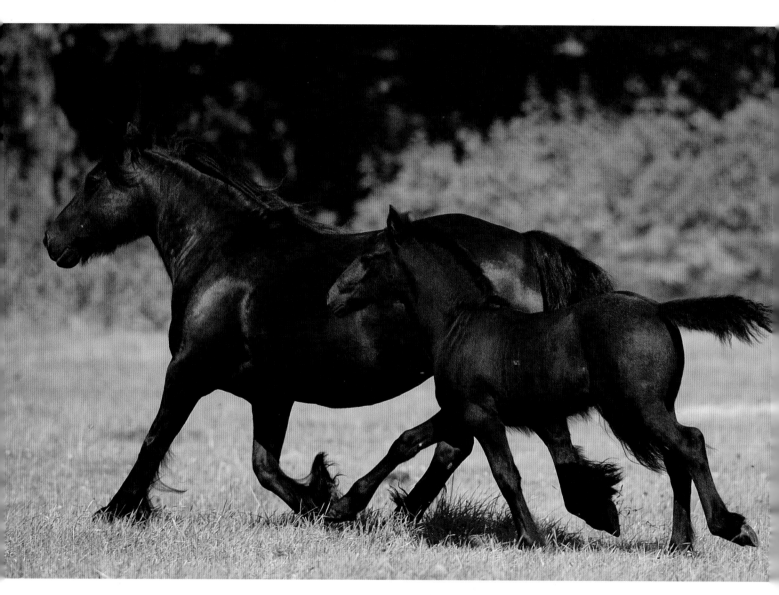

Above Although bay, brown and sometimes grey Fell ponies can be seen, the breed is generally black, thought to be as a result of Friesian influence.

Right The Fell is similar to the Dales, but stands slightly smaller at around 14hh. It has the same luxuriant mane and tail.

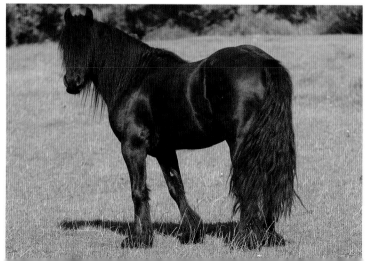

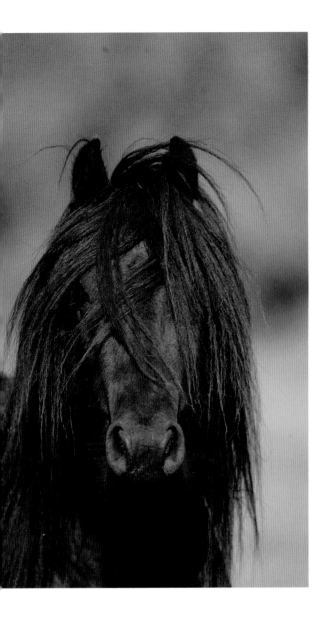

Fell

A close relative of the Dales, the Fell pony takes its name from the old Norse word for hill and is found in the western Pennines. Along with the Exmoor pony, it is considered to be the purest of the British breeds. As is the case with the Dales, its descendants were the early Celtic pony mixed with the foreign stock imported in Roman times. Among the stock brought to Britain by the Romans were Friesian horses. Compact and well made, an estimated 1,000 of these light draught-type equines were left behind when the invaders withdrew to return to their besieged city. The Fell is a Friesian in miniature and has its swift, ground-covering trot.

With the Industrial Revolution, the Fell found its niche as a pack pony, carrying wool, copper, lead and coal across northern England. It worked in the coalmines, ferrying machinery and goods above ground as well as working below ground when the height of the mines allowed.

The Fell Pony Society was set up in 1922 to ensure the purity of the breed. The modern breed differs little from its ancient ancestors, and remains in demand as a riding and driving pony. The Queen's husband, the Duke of Edinburgh, drove a team of Fell ponies with international success.

Above The Fell has a chiselled head and neat pony ears. The breed generally displays a lively intelligence.

Welsh Section A/B

Ponies have roamed the Welsh mountains for thousands of years, and during that time have developed a hardiness and intelligence that have made them popular the world over. On his invasion of Britain, Julius Caesar was said to be impressed by the native ponies.

In the 16th century, when King Henry VIII ordered the destruction of any equine standing at less than 15hh (page 97), only the ponies in the most inaccessible parts of the country were able to survive, among them those that roamed high in the Welsh mountains. Due to the harsh weather conditions and poor grazing, the Welsh Mountain pony (section A of the Welsh studbook) developed into a tough little animal with a wily intelligence. Despite the fact that other breeds have influenced it, the Welsh Mountain pony retains its physical characteristics and the breed has been used to improve other stock.

There is unarguably Arab blood in the Welsh Mountain pony; it can clearly be seen in the breed's concave or dished profile. It is likely that the Oriental-type horses were brought to the British Isles by Caesar and his invading armies, and left behind when they retreated. The Welsh pony (section B of the studbook), is slightly larger than the Welsh Mountain pony, and has more quality and freer action. It makes an ideal riding pony for children.

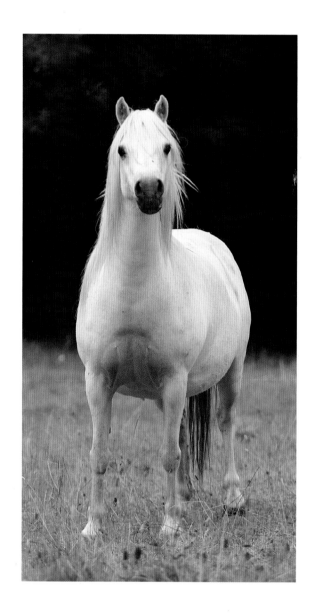

Above Grey is a common coat colour in the Welsh Mountain pony, although all other solid colours do occur.

Opposite This enchanting Welsh Mountain foal has the characteristic broad forehead and dished face of the breed.

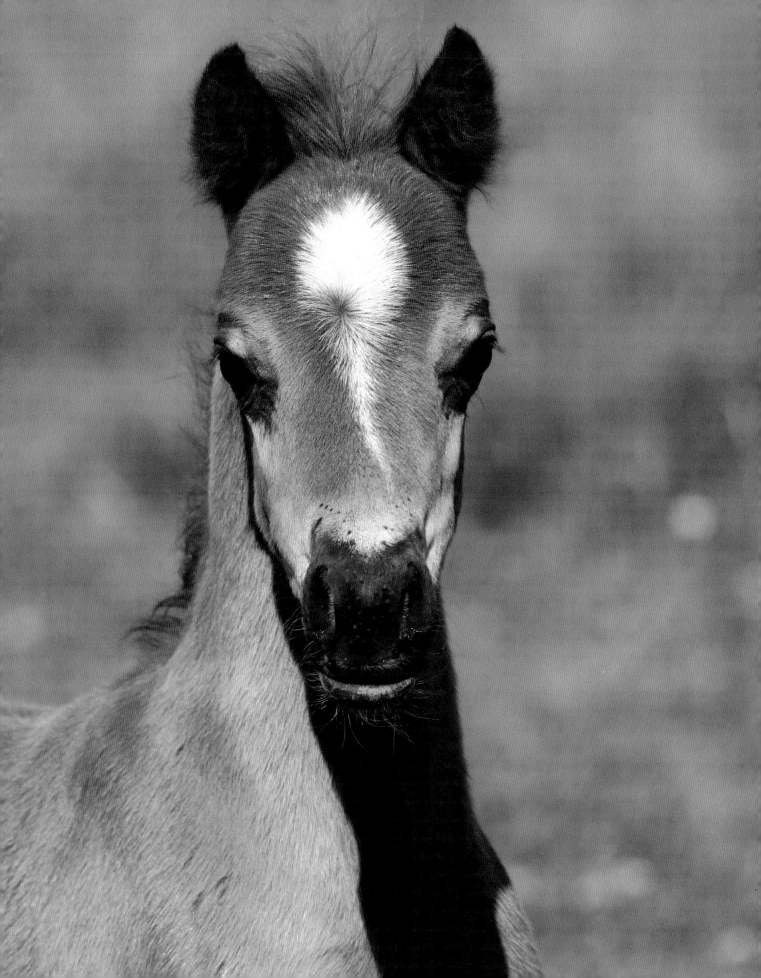

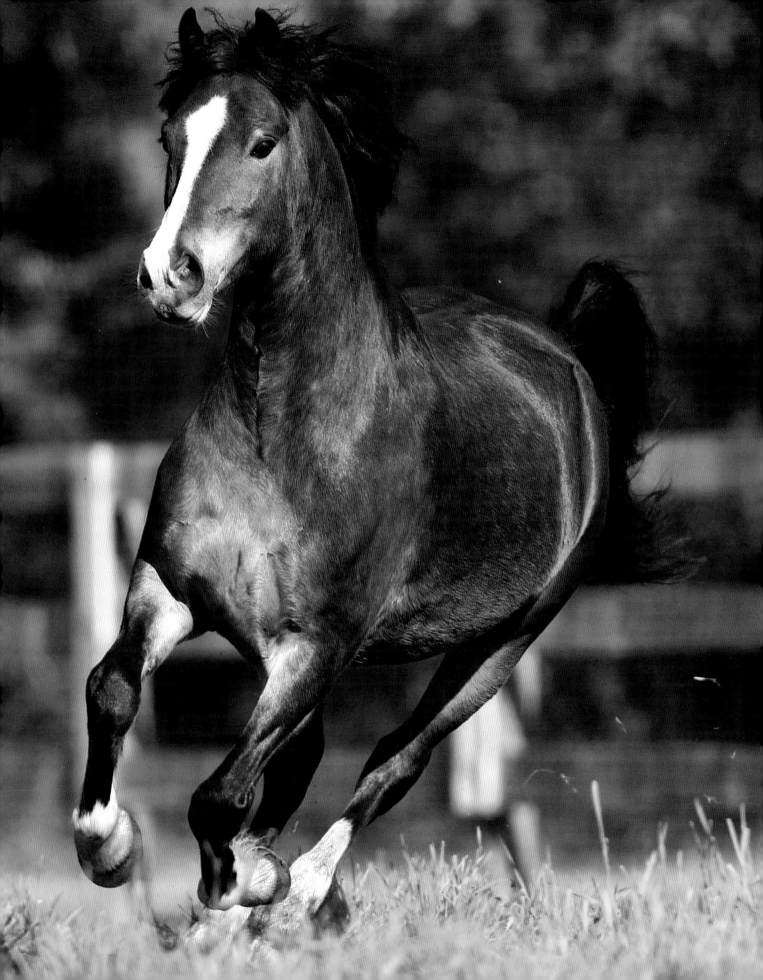

Welsh Section C/D

In medieval times the Welsh Cob (section D of the studbook) – called a 'rouncey' – was used to lead the massive warhorses known as 'destriers', whose natural gait was the trot. The smaller Welsh Cob had to be able to match the destriers stride by stride, and even today the Welsh Cob is renowned for its active, powerful trot.

Henry Tudor attained the English throne with the help of the Welsh military mounted on fleet-footed and tough Cobs. The horse has always been valued by the British Army for the mounted infantry, as well as for pulling heavy artillery and equipment. Until the late 20th century the War Office paid premiums for the best Welsh Cob stallions. Before motorization the Welsh Cob was also used as the speediest means of transport for doctors and tradesmen. A test would be to trot a horse from Cardiff to Dowlais, 35 miles uphill – the fastest horses could do this in less than three hours, never changing pace. Many believe there was Welsh Cob blood in the original Justin Morgan horse (page 116), which would certainly explain his power and speed.

It is said that in silhouette the Welsh Cob should look like a scaled up version of the Welsh section A, with the same pony head and quality. There is no upper height limit for Welsh Cobs. The Welsh pony of Cob type (section C of the studbook) should stand at no higher than 13.2hh.

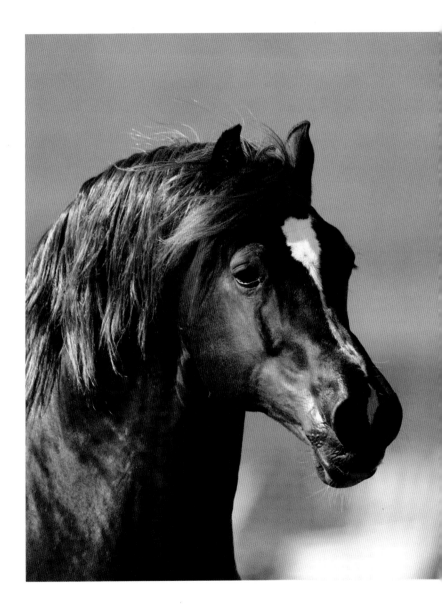

Opposite A Welsh Section C shows off the active paces for which the breed is renowned.

Above All the might and power of the Welsh Section D can be seen in this magnificent stallion's head and neck.

Irish Draught

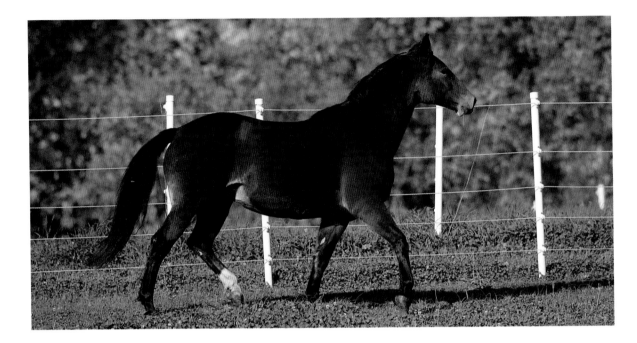

Despite its name the Irish Draught is not a heavy horse breed. Its history is that of an all-rounder – a horse that could work on the farm, pull the cart and take the farmer hunting. Indeed, most people consider the best sort of hunter to be a Thoroughbred crossed with an Irish Draught. Sadly, this has in some ways been the breed's undoing, for the clamour for TB-ID crosses has resulted in comparatively few pure ID horses and the breed has more than once almost been lost.

The Irish Draught's origins are, like the origins of many breeds, those of a warhorse. The *Cúchulainn Cycle*, written more than 2,000 years ago, describes horses pulling chariots; these horses appear to be remarkably similar to the modern Irish Draught. Anglo-Norman blood came in the 12th century, followed by Spanish blood in the 16th century, when Ireland traded with Spain.

The Irish Draught served on the front lines in times of war, and served its masters equally well in peacetime. However, during periods of poverty and famine Irish breeders did not register their horses and many were lost. The Irish Draught Horse Society was founded in 1976 to preserve the breed, but there are still only an estimated 2,000 pure-bred Irish Draughts worldwide.

Above Although the Irish Draught is strong and well built, it is not a heavy horse breed as its name may suggest. It is typified by clean shoulders, a powerful back, a sloping croup and plenty of good, flat bone.

Opposite Most solid colours appear in the Irish Draught – the speckled coat of the horse shown here is known as 'flea-bitten grey'.

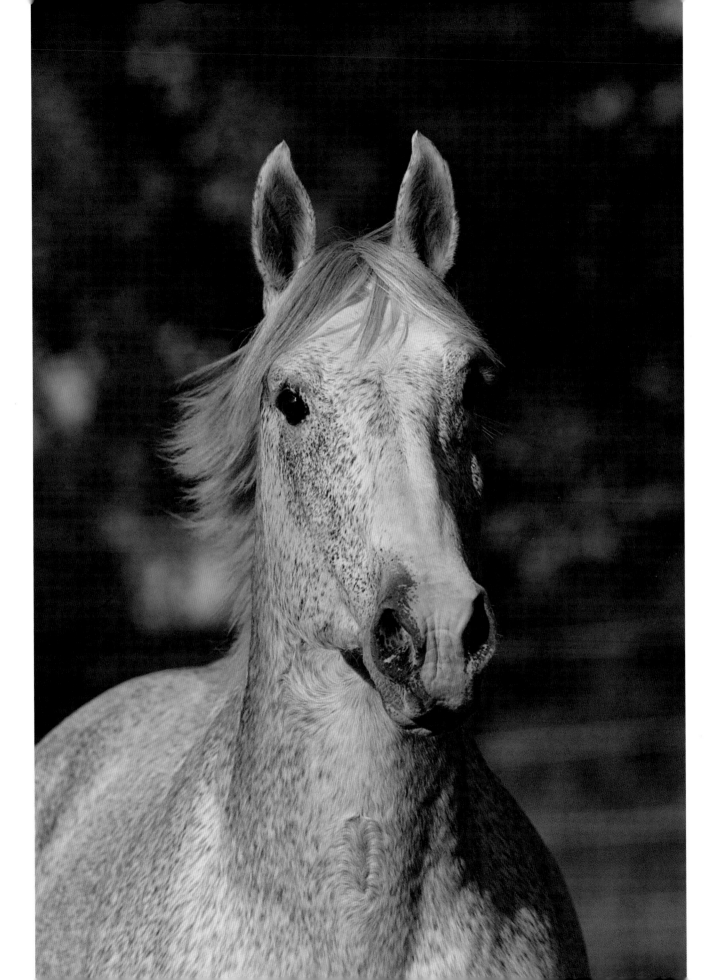

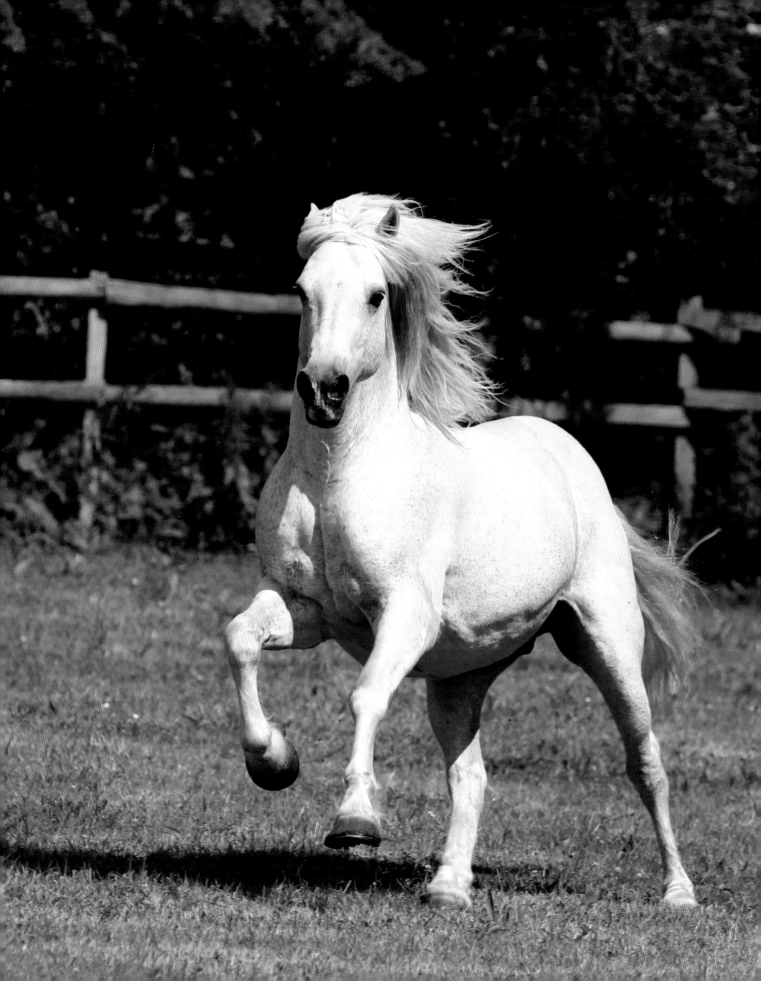

Connemara

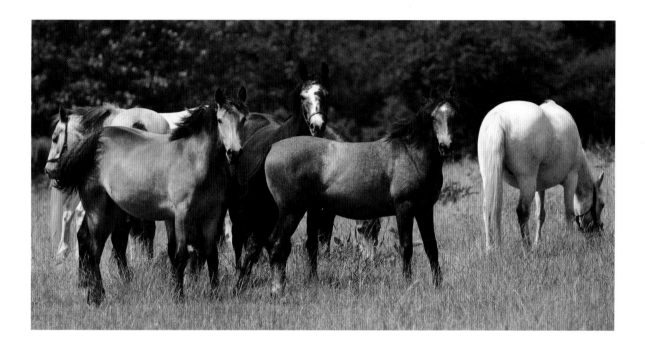

Western Ireland is rocky and barren, and its coastline is pounded by the raging Atlantic Ocean. For any creature to survive on this almost lunar landscape, it must be rugged indeed. Connemara ponies based on the tough little horses introduced by Celtic warriors to pull their carts and chariots have lived here for centuries. A theory is that when the Spanish Armada was wrecked off the western coast in the 16th century, some of the horses swam ashore and mated with the local stock. Considered to be Ireland's only native breed, the Connemara has certainly been influenced by both Arab and Thoroughbred blood.

The farmers of the region, themselves having to struggle to survive, captured and tamed the wild ponies, and found them to be excellent all-rounders. They would select a mare, which would give them a foal each year to sell and serve them well as a working horse. It could carry turf from the bogs for cooking, bear seaweed for fertilizing crops and haul rocks to clear the land for agriculture. The sturdy pony was strong enough to carry these loads, sound enough to keep going through the mud and enduring enough to pull the cart to church on a Sunday. While their lot has undoubtedly improved, today's Connemara ponies remain supreme all-rounders.

Opposite The beauty of the Connemara make it as successful in the showring as it is in most equestrian disciplines.

Above Dun, roan and grey are all common coat colours in the Connemara; the dun may well give away the breed's Spanish heritage.

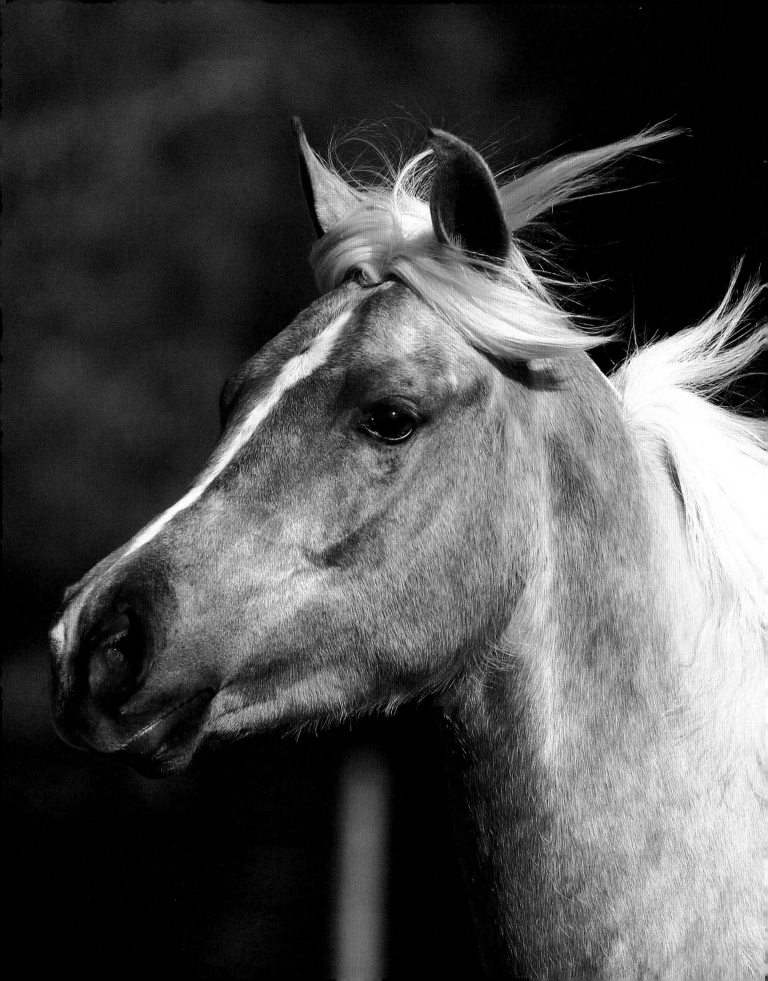

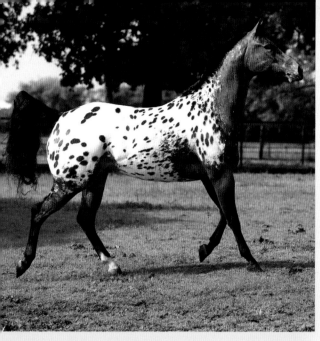

The Americas

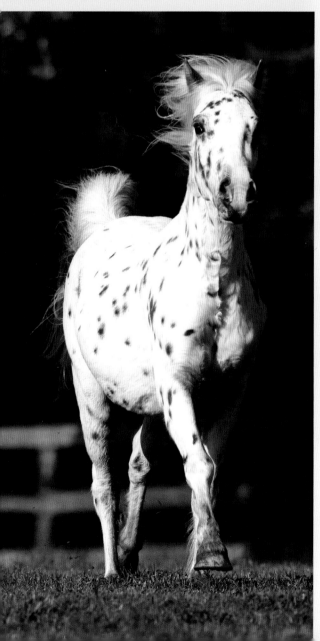

No one knows why the early horses died out completely in North America after the last Ice Age, although it is generally accepted that *Equus* evolved there. That the United States' equines are today so plentiful and so diverse is a credit to generations of American horse breeders.

Clockwise from far left Quarter Horse (page 112); Appaloosa (page 123); Pony of the Americas (page 119).

Quarter Horse

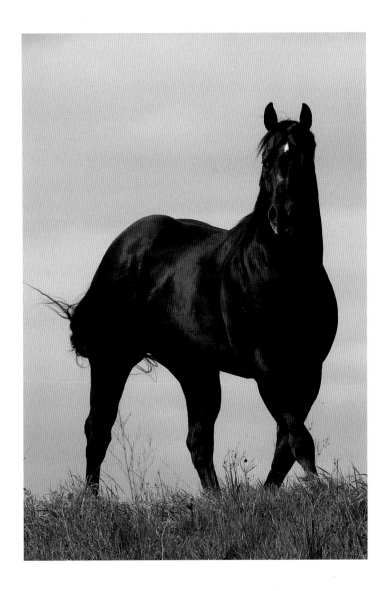

There is a common misconception that the name of this American breed derives from the fact that it was 25 per cent Thoroughbred. In fact, it was named for the distance – a quarter of a mile – over which it raced, often with wagers for enormous sums on its nose. Small and compact, the Quarter Horse could cover this short distance faster than any other equine, and the swiftest individuals are still named Celebrated American Running Horses. It is said that some of the great plantations changed ownership on the result of a race. The official breed name, American Quarter Horse, was formerly registered in 1940. The first known Quarter Horse races, however, were held in Enrico County, Virginia, in 1674, when one-on-one matches were run down village streets.

The Quarter Horse has the distinction of being generally accepted as the oldest true American breed. It was, however, almost lost. Before its registry, no proper breeding records were kept, and the introduction of the English Thoroughbred to America resulted in sprint racing falling out of favour as courses were built for longer distance contests. However, the Quarter Horse also possessed 'cow sense', making it a favourite with ranch hands. It remains popular today in rodeos and as a recreational riding horse.

Above Compact and well made, this handsome Quarter Horse has the desirable sloping shoulder that gives it freedom of movement.

Opposite This tiny foal will grow to be as big and strong as its mother, standing at around 15.2hh at maturity.

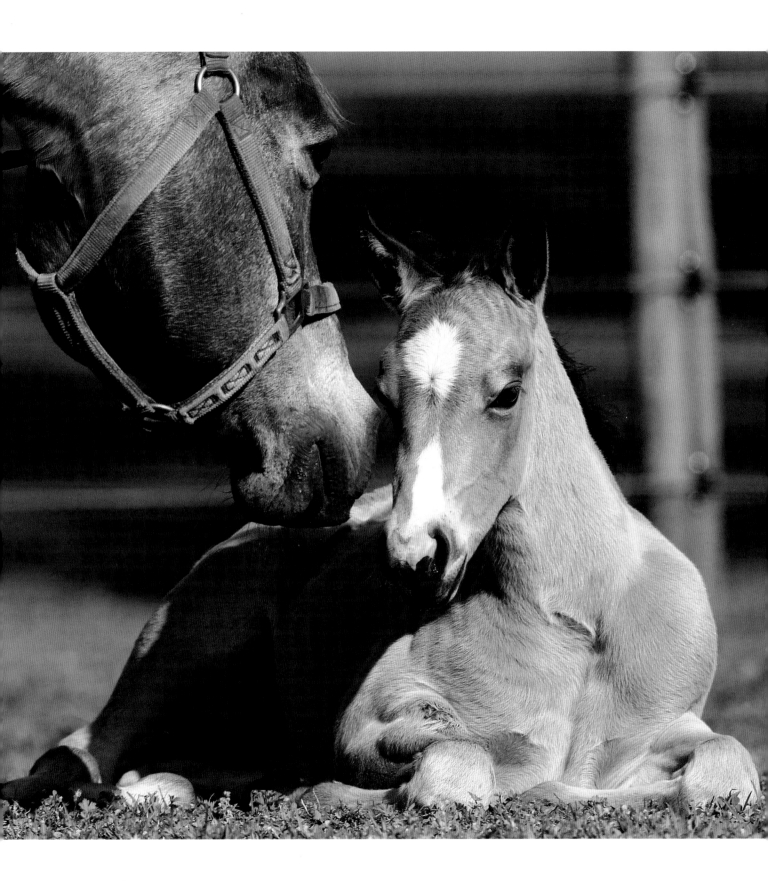

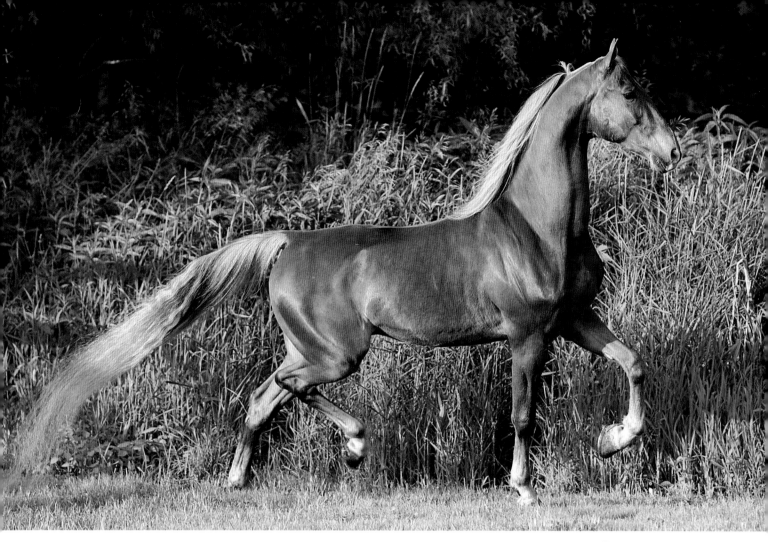

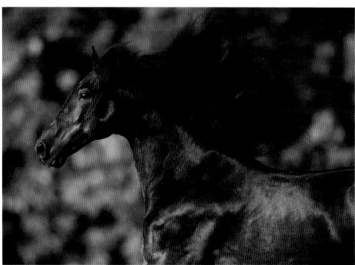

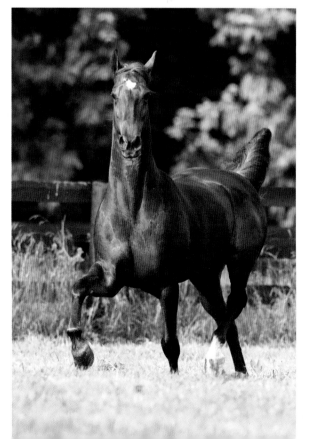

Top The ideal American Saddlebred is well proportioned and graceful; it is a superb all-rounder.

Above The breed has the lean good looks of a Thoroughbred and carries its head high on its arching neck.

American Saddlebred

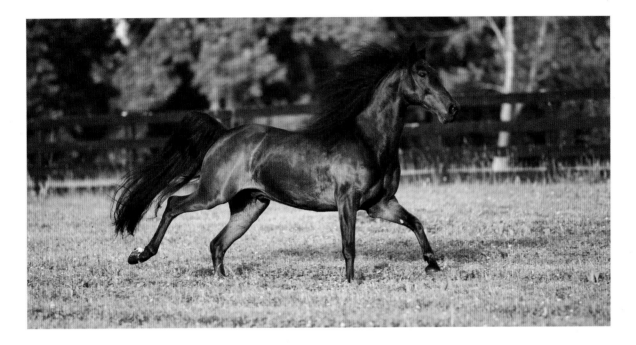

Based on Galloway and Hobby Horses imported from Britain, as well as the Thoroughbreds that came later, the American Saddlebred combines the good looks of a Thoroughbred with the easy gaits of a pacer. In the early 19th century it was known simply as the 'American Horse'. Kind and willing, and handsome and strong, it was the ideal all-rounder – it could pull a carriage as easily as a plough and was comfortable to ride.

In the American Civil War the breed was the mount of choice of the generals due to its endurance and courage – the men of Nathan Bedford Forest and John Morgan Hunt rode Saddlebreds. General Robert E. Lee's Traveller, perhaps the most renowned horse of the Civil War, was the epitome of a Saddlebred. By the Thoroughbred Gray Eagle out of a mare of mixed breeding, Traveller is said to have possessed a natural smooth rack, a lateral four-beat gait with all four legs moving independently, which is extremely comfortable for the rider. When the Civil War ended the American Saddlebred spread across the United States as the soldiers returned home along with their horses, with whom they had endured so much. The Saddlebred's fame then spread further afield, its reputation as a beautiful, amenable and intelligent equine preceding it.

Opposite Elegant and refined, this American Saddlebred mare shows why the breed excels in the showring.

Above The breed is generally chestnut and stands at around 16hh. It is popular for its smooth, elastic paces as well as its beauty.

Morgan

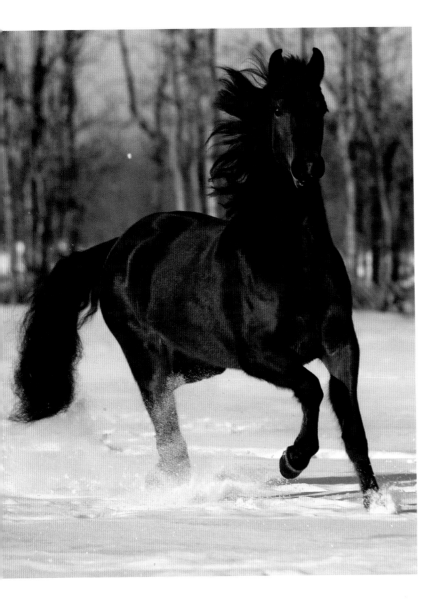

Such was the popularity of the original 'Justin Morgan horse' that even those who lost money in bets against him cheered his achievements. Justin Morgan himself, a businessman and horseman who moved to Randolph, Vermont, acquired what was to prove the founding sire of one of North America's most important horse breeds as a foal in 1789. The colt, whom he named Figure, was compact and strong, and possessed good looks, exceptional movement and an equable temperament.

Justin Morgan used horses, including Figure, to plough his fields; Figure soon proved stronger than many of the draught horses, despite his relatively diminutive stature. He was also victorious in the trotting and running races that were popular at the time. His speed, hardiness, endurance and pure determination became renowned, and soon there were few who would bet against 'the Morgan horse'.

The horse's fame spread and before long owners of mares were sending their broodmares to be covered by the Morgan horse. Figure – whose breeding was probably based on Thoroughbred, Arab and Welsh Cob lines – stamped his progeny with his good looks and temperament, and the new breed was born. Figure proved to have longevity, too – he died at the age of 32 from an untreated wound after being kicked by another horse. All modern Morgans can be traced back to him.

Above The Morgan stands at around 14.2hh and is as hardy as it is beautiful. It is spirited and lively, with a keen intelligence.

Opposite Morgans are compact, well-built and refined in appearance, with expressive faces and well-arched necks. These two individuals are play fighting.

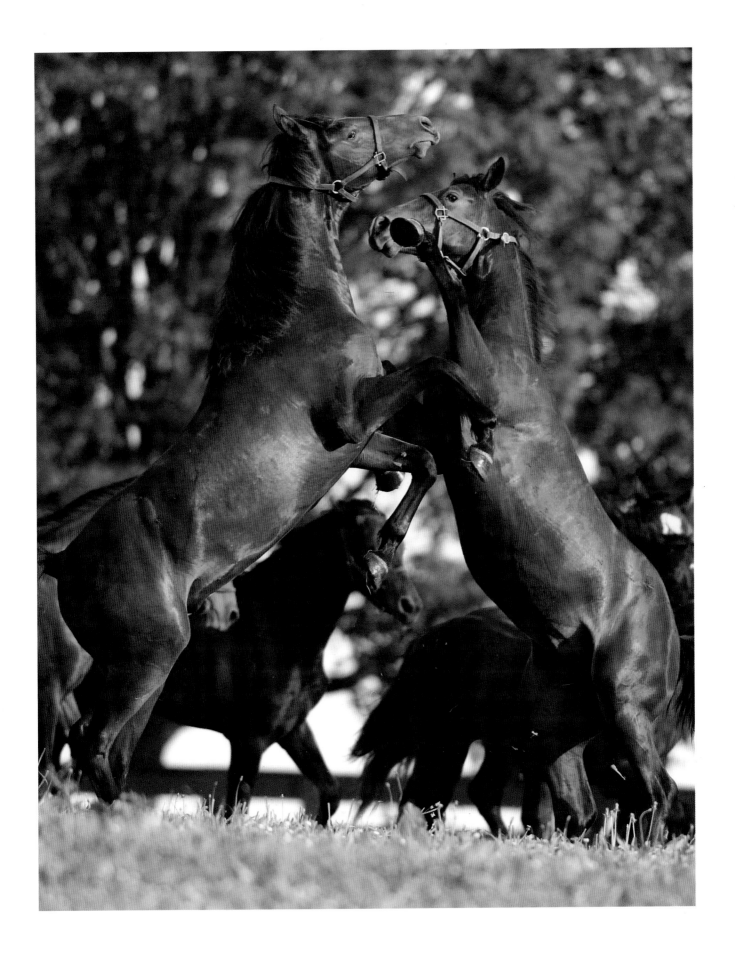

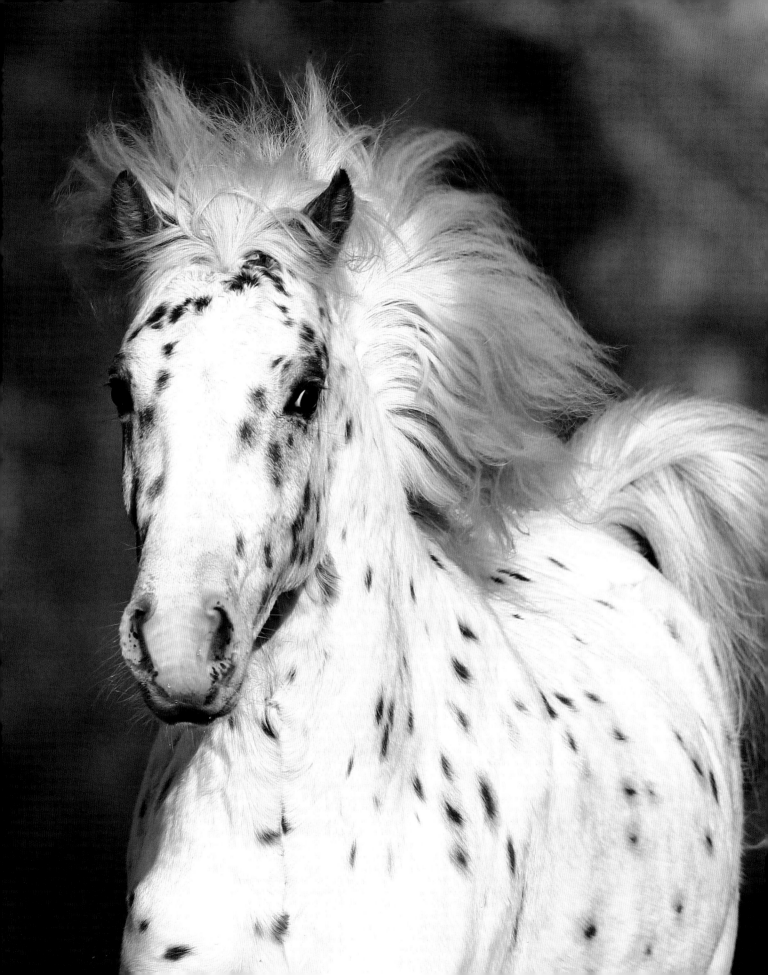

Pony of the Americas

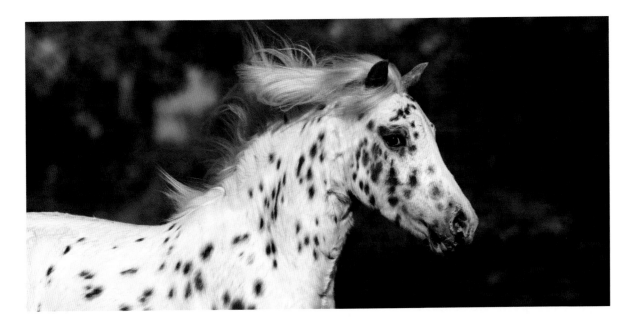

A mark like a handprint was to be the basis for the United States' eponymous pony breed. In 1954 a Shetland pony breeder was offered an Arab-Appaloosa mare that had accidentally been covered by a Shetland stallion. Les Boomhower, a lawyer from Mason City, Iowa, agreed to take the mare and her offspring after she foaled. Her colt was marked with what appeared to be a black handprint on his flank. Boomhower was enchanted by the mark and named the colt Black Hand. He was to become the foundation sire of the Pony of the Americas, or POA.

Boomhower set up the registry with fellow breeders, forming the POA Club. The aim was to breed a quality pony of fixed type suitable for children. It had to stand at 11–13hh, and to have an attractive head, preferably slightly dished like that of an Arab, and distinctive Appaloosa markings – most importantly, these markings must be visible at a distance of 40 feet.

Appaloosas were initially used to provide the coat patterns and Shetlands the small size, but a variety of other horse breeds have since been added to the mix. These include the Quarter Horse, Welsh pony, Thoroughbred, Mustang and Arab. There are thought to be around 50,000 POAs in 'clubs' all over the United States. The size of the breed has increased, but the emphasis remains on both quality and fun.

Opposite The Pony of the Americas displays characteristics such as a short-coupled body, legs in proportion and a pretty head.

Above The Pony of the Americas is attractive and full of quality, wth a neat head set on a well-carried, slightly arched neck, which is of medium length.

Standardbred

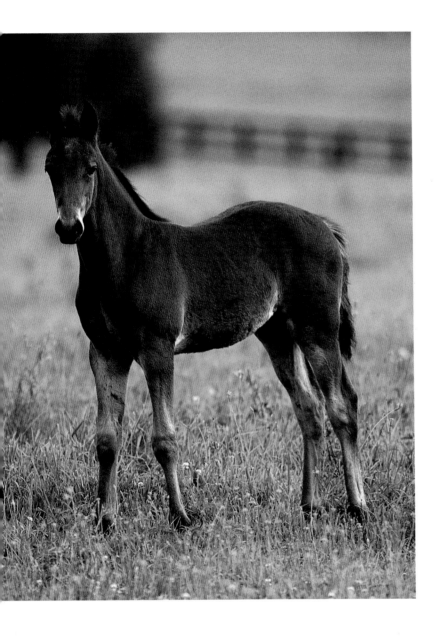

Everyone is familiar with the lively refrain of *Camptown Races*. The 'bob-tailed nag' of the song was a Standardbred named Flora Temple, although it is unlikely that she ever competed on a 'racetrack five miles long', as in the lyrics. The breed became known as the Standardbred because the horses were developed to race one mile in a standard time. This distance is still standard in almost every harness race. The early trotting races – pacers did not come until later – were contested along city roads, which were cleared for these head-to-head challenges. Today many American cities still have a Race Street.

A stallion named Messenger, an English Thoroughbred, was to form the basis of the breed. Foaled in 1780, he was the great-grandsire of Hambletonian 10, back to whom the heritage of every modern Standardbred can be traced. The renowned Flora Temple – who had been docked as a foal, hence 'bob-tail' – won 92 races and was second 14 times over a nine-year period. She equalled or beat the world record six times, and was the first horse to break the 2-minute 20-second mile. In 1858 she was valued at $8,000. Then came the pacer – the first to break the 2-minute mile was Star Pointer, in 1897. The horse credited with popularizing pacing was Dan Patch, who recorded a 1-minute 55-second mile in 1906 and as a result became one of the most famous ever Standardbreds.

Above This elegant Standardbred foal already has the length of limb that is characteristic of the breed.

Opposite top The Standardbred's refined but plain head is straight, with large nostrils and a broad forehead.

Opposite below A dramatic burst of speed points to this Standardbred's heritage as a supreme racehorse.

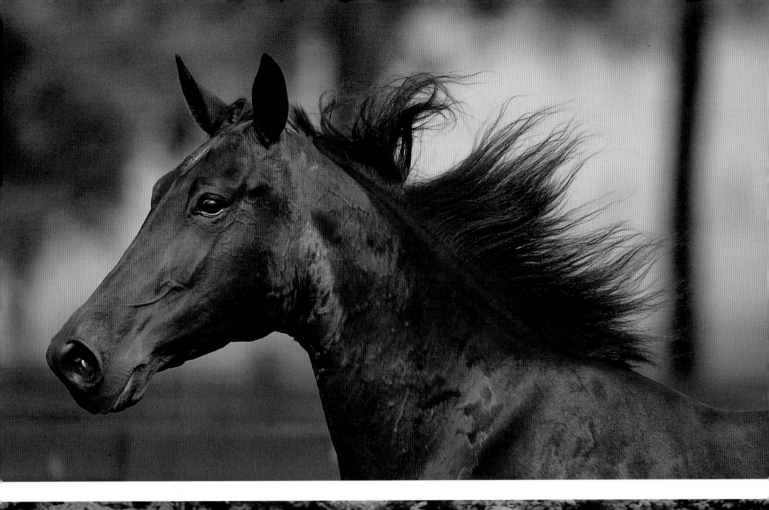
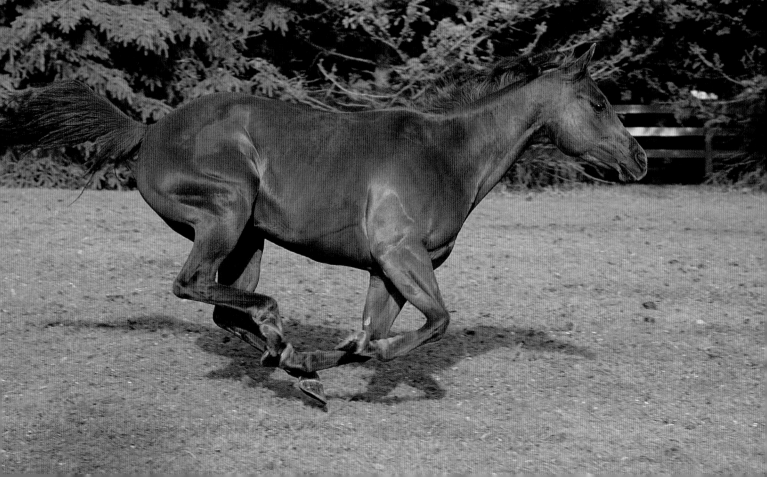

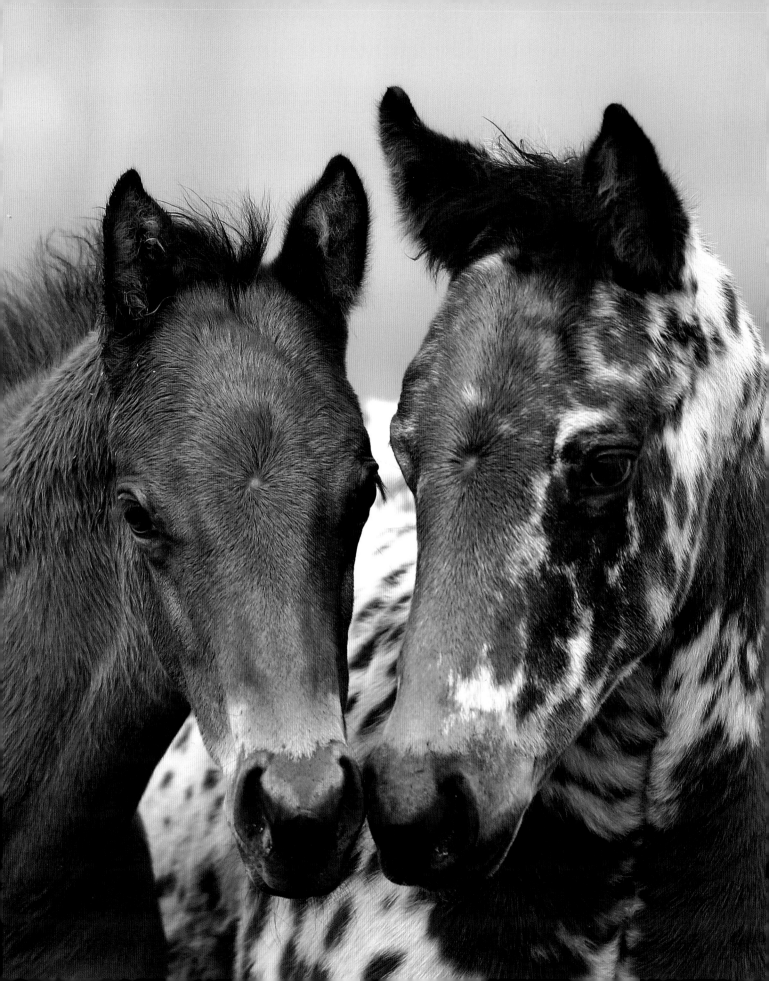

Appaloosa

As American as the Stars and Stripes, the beautiful Appaloosa is arguably one of the most iconic breeds. It is believed that its name derived from the Palouse river – as in, 'it's a Palousey horse' – in the region where it was the first horse to be selectively bred by Native American tribes. Both the spotted coat of the Appaloosa and its speed and endurance were highly prized by the Nez Perce people. The breed was, however, almost lost forever when the white settlers imposed land treaties and claimed the fertile region around the Palouse, which ran through North Idaho. A battle at White Bird Canyon in June 1877 marked the beginning of a war between the native tribes and settlers. The Nez Perce surrendered in October and, having confiscated their horses, the government of the United States prohibited the tribe from owning Appaloosa horses – a law that was not repealed until 1991. Today the tribe keeps a small herd on the Lapwai reservation in Idaho.

After the tribe's surrender the breed was diluted due to indiscriminate breeding, but a wheat farmer named Claude Thompson recognized the beauty of the spotted horses. In 1938 he formed the Appaloosa Horse Club with just a handful of stock.

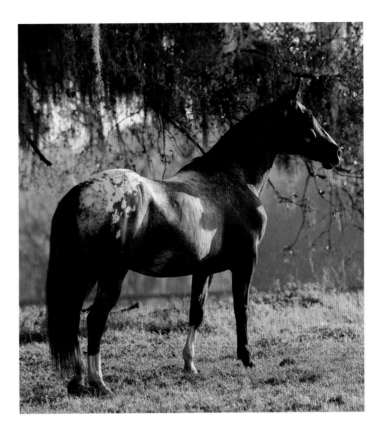

While the spotted coat of the Appaloosa is its most renowned feature, the breed shows other traits that are equally important – mottled skin, white sclera around the eyes and striped hooves.

Opposite The white sclera is visible around the eye of the Appaloosa foal on the right; this is regarded as a desired trait.

Above This Appaloosa has white splodges on a coloured background rather than dark spots – there are seven recognized coat colours.

Tennessee Walking Horse

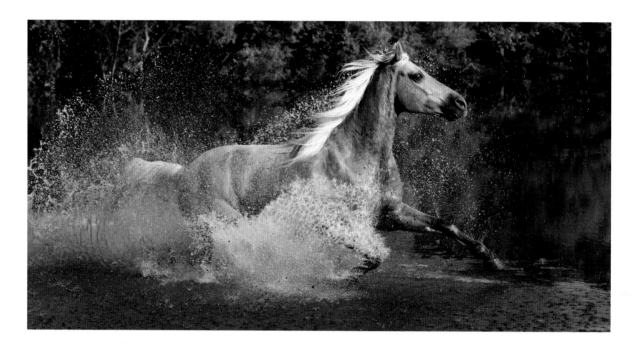

The Tennessee Walking Horse has two claims to fame: it is the first American breed to bear the name of a state, and its flashy, high-stepping gait is supremely comfortable. Founded in the Bluegrass region of Tennessee, the Walker is the result of combining several horse breeds, including the now-extinct Narragansett Pacer, as well as the Canadian Pacer, Morgan, Standardbred, Thoroughbred and American Saddlebred.

Originally bred as a utility horse, the Walker earned a reputation as a smooth, speedy and sure-footed transport over the hills and valleys of its rocky home state. The breed was additionally very good-looking, intelligent and willing. Its foundation sire is designated as a colt called Black Allan, foaled in 1886 as a result of a mating between a trotting stallion called Allendorf and Maggie Marshall, a Morgan mare.

The paces for which the Tennessee Walking Horse became famous are primarily the flat-foot walk, running walk and canter, all of which are inherited rather than taught. The most desirable of these is the running walk, a smooth, gliding gait at which the horse can travel at up to 20 miles per hour. It is also able to perform the rack, stepping pace, fox trot, single-foot and other easy trail-riding gaits.

Above The agile Tennessee Walking Horse has clean, sloping shoulders that allow it to move freely through all the gaits.

Opposite The Tennessee Walking Horse typically has a long neck, large but refined head and small, well-placed ears.

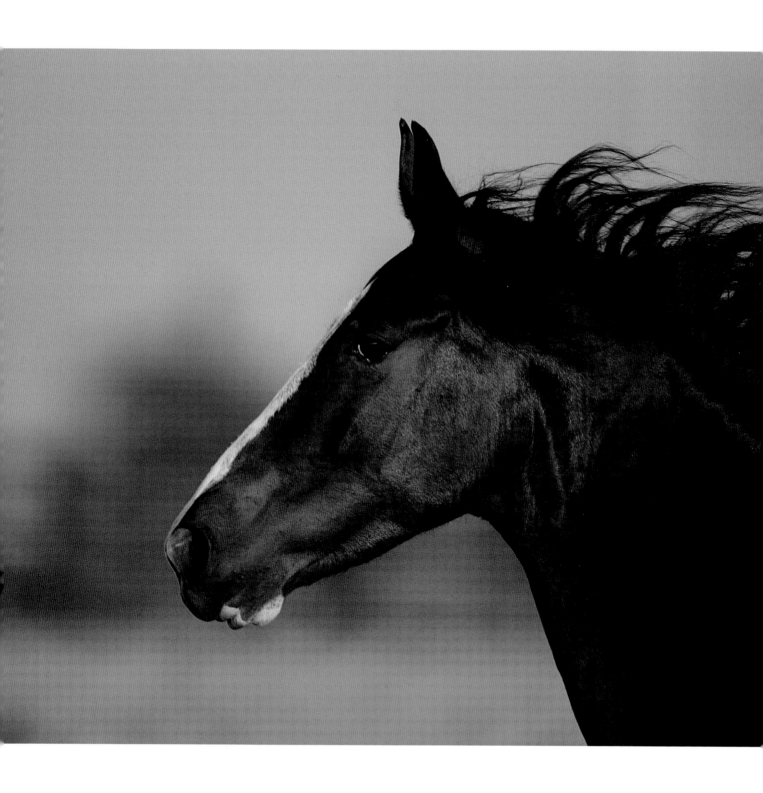

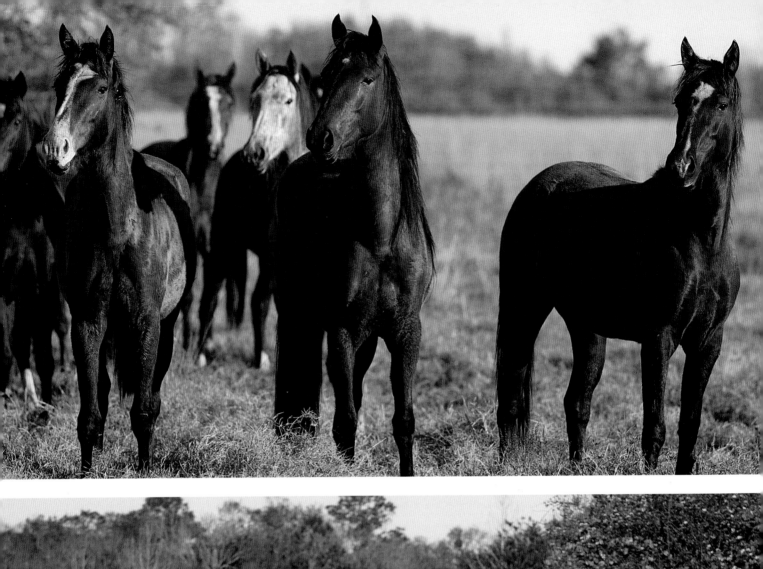
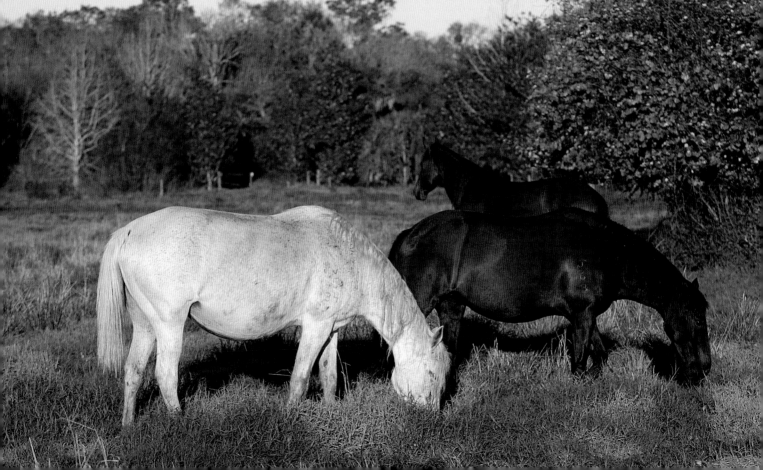

Florida Cracker

A rawhide whip whistles through the air, snapped back by its expert handler with a sharp 'crack'. This defining sound gave the Florida cowboys and the little horses they rode the name 'cracker'. The cattle industry in Florida that gave rise to these horses was developed more than 500 years ago and still flourishes today.

Like the Mustang's heritage, that of the Florida Cracker is essentially Spanish. The horse is neatly made and agile, with an innate 'cow sense' that made it supreme for working cattle. It was often referred to as the Florida Cow Pony, but it had many names over the years, including Seminole Pony, Marsh Tackie, Prairie Pony and Grass Cut.

With the Great Depression of the 1930s, the cattle and those that tended them in the Dust Bowl of Colorado, Kansas, Oklahoma and Texas moved into Florida. They brought with them an unwelcome guest – the screwworm, which parasitizes cattle. This changed forever the way that cattle were worked – instead of being herded and driven, they had to be roped, then held for treatment to get rid of the parasite. The agile Florida Cracker fell out of favour to the bigger, stronger Quarter Horse and the breed was almost lost. It was only due to the efforts of ranching families, who continued to breed Florida Crackers and whose perseverance retained vital bloodlines, that the breed was saved from extinction.

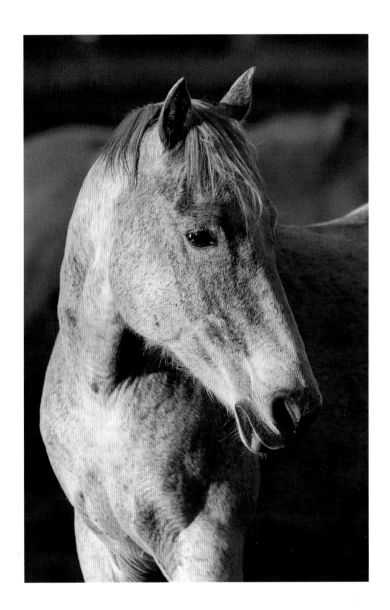

Opposite top The Florida Cracker is finely built and agile, standing at little over 14.2hh.

Opposite below Tough and hardy, the Florida Cracker is an easy keeper that is well suited to ranching life.

Above The Florida Cracker has a refined head with a straight or concave profile and alert and intelligent eye.

Missouri Fox Trotter

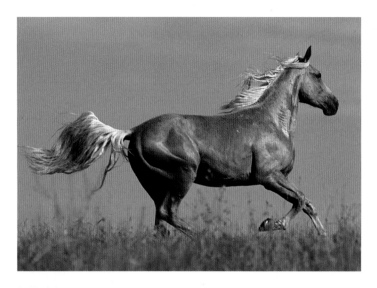

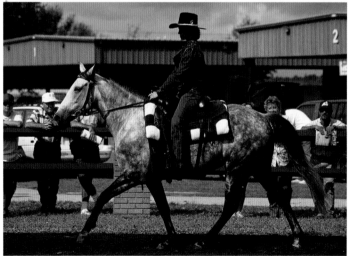

A horse that is every bit as delightful as its name, the Missouri Fox Trotter danced across the rugged Ozark Mountains with the first settlers of the new state. Missouri was given statehood in 1821 and was settled by pioneers who streamed across the Mississippi from Kentucky, Tennessee and Virginia. They brought their equines with them, a mix of Arab, Morgan and plantation horses from the Deep South, together with gaited stock such as the Tennessee Walking Horse, all of which were used to develop the Fox Trotter.

The breed was both comfortable to ride and very surefooted, and consequently ideally suited to the mountainous state. Its signature gait, a diagonal, fluid, four-beat fox trot, allowed it to travel long distances at a steady, smooth speed. In the fox trot, the horse appears to walk with its front legs and trot behind, so the rider experiences very little jarring, as the hind feet slide into place. The Fox Trotter can move at speeds of 5–8 miles an hour.

With its gentle nature, the Fox Trotter proved a most versatile horse. It could do almost any job required around the homestead, including ploughing, pulling logs and working cattle, and was smart enough to pull a buggy. It became renowned as the 'common man's pleasure horse', and is popular today as a riding and show horse.

Top The Missouri Fox Trotter is elegant and refined, and the paces for which it is famous are extremely comfortable.

Above The lateral gait of the Fox Trotter results in there being very little jarring for the rider.

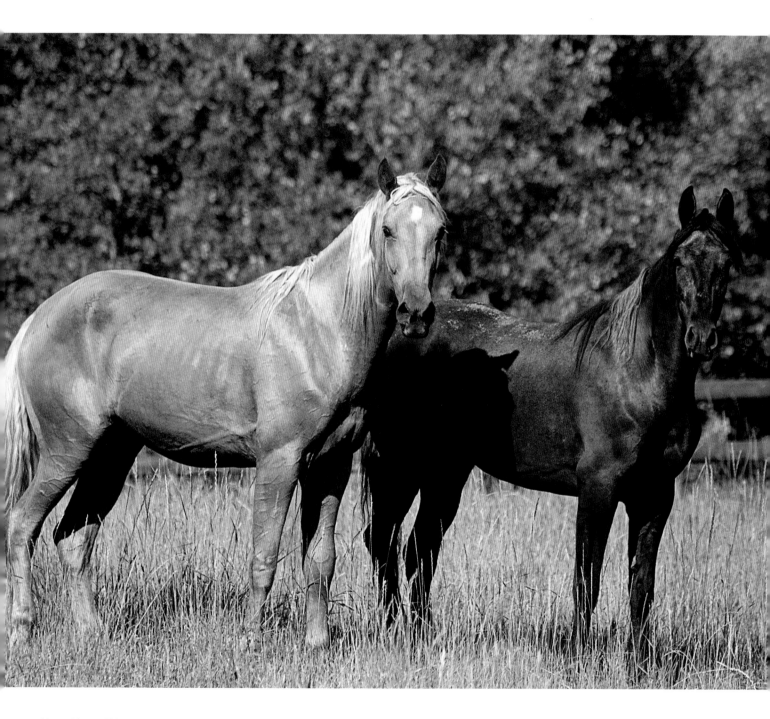

Above Most solid colours can be seen in the
Missouri Fox Trotter, the palomino (shown left)
being an indicator of Spanish ancestry.

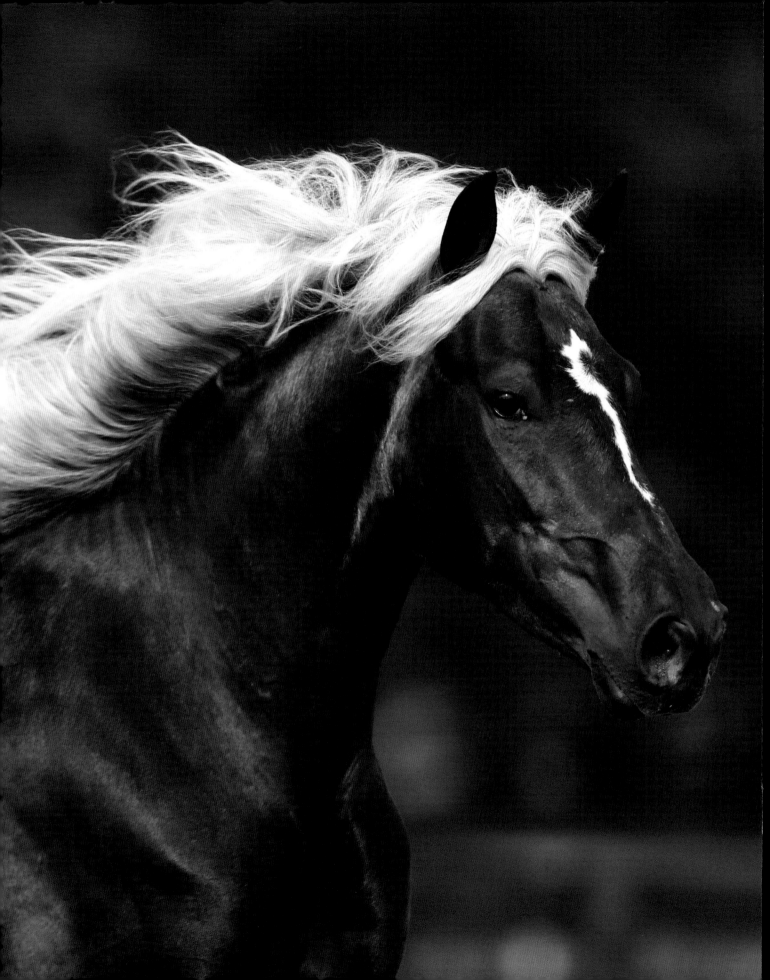

Rocky Mountain Horse

A farmer called Sam Tuttle is credited with the recognition of the Rocky Mountain breed, but the horse that founded the strain is something of a legend. The story goes that a young colt, thought to be around two years old, appeared in the foothills of the mountains of Eastern Kentucky some time around 1890. Although its origins are unknown, it was referred to by the local people as 'the Rocky Mountain Horse'. The name was to stick.

Rocky Mountain Horses were gentle of nature, easy keepers and willing workers, and possessed an easy, four-beat gait well suited to the rugged terrain of the Appalachians. The people of the region were not wealthy, so a horse had to be able to do a variety of different jobs. A horse here was not a luxury but a necessity.

Sam Tuttle, of Spout Springs, Kentucky, had the concession for horseback riding in the Natural Bridge State Park. He found the Rocky Mountain to be the ideal mount for those of nervous disposition who rode the rough mountain trails. His most treasured stallion was Old Tobe, who sired horses up to the age of 34 and died at the age of 37. Many Rocky

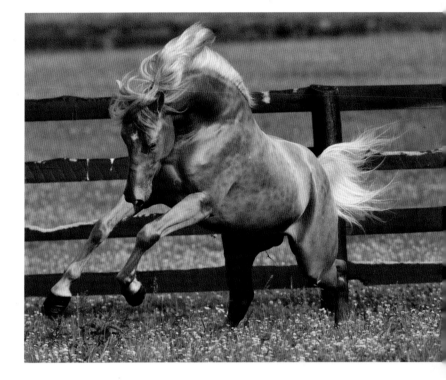

Mountains still carry his bloodlines. Old Tobe passed on his sweet temper and comfortable gaits to continue a line of equines known universally as 'a horse for all seasons'.

Opposite The original Rocky Mountain Horse was thought to have been chocolate-brown with a silver mane and tail.

Above The Rocky Mountain Horse is typically surefooted, agile and athletic, and its spirit is complemented by a calm intelligence.

Palomino

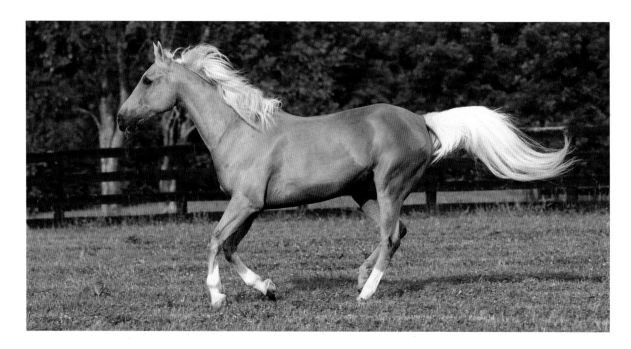

The glowing golden Palomino horse breed was introduced to the Americas via Spanish stock, but the palomino horse coat colour is thought to be as old as the horse itself. It was known to be popular with Spain's Queen Isabella (1474–1504), and is still sometimes described as 'Isabella' today. Palomino horses are depicted in paintings and tapestries dating back centuries. A light gold-coloured horse can, for instance, be seen in Botticelli's *The Adoration of the Magi*, which was painted in 1475 and now hangs in the National Gallery in Washington DC. They also feature in many artistic and literary works across Asia, Europe, China and Japan.

A true Palomino should be the colour of a newly minted 14-carat gold coin, although it may vary from light to dark. The skin beneath is usually grey, not pink, and the mane and tail must be white.

Although technically palomino is a colour rather than a breed, the Palomino is recognized as a breed in the United States. The breed association, Palomino Horse Breeders of America, was established in 1941 to register and improve the breed and to fix a type of quality saddle horse standing at 14–17hh. The golden horse remains popular, with the most assured breeding to produce a Palomino being between that of a cremello and a chestnut.

Above The glowing gold coat colour of the Palomino makes it stand out in the showring, and it is much sought after as a parade horse.

Opposite The Palomino is usually the colour of a gold coin, as here, although a wider colour range is often accepted. Interestingly, the gold coat colour and pale mane and tail were seen in equines in ancient China.

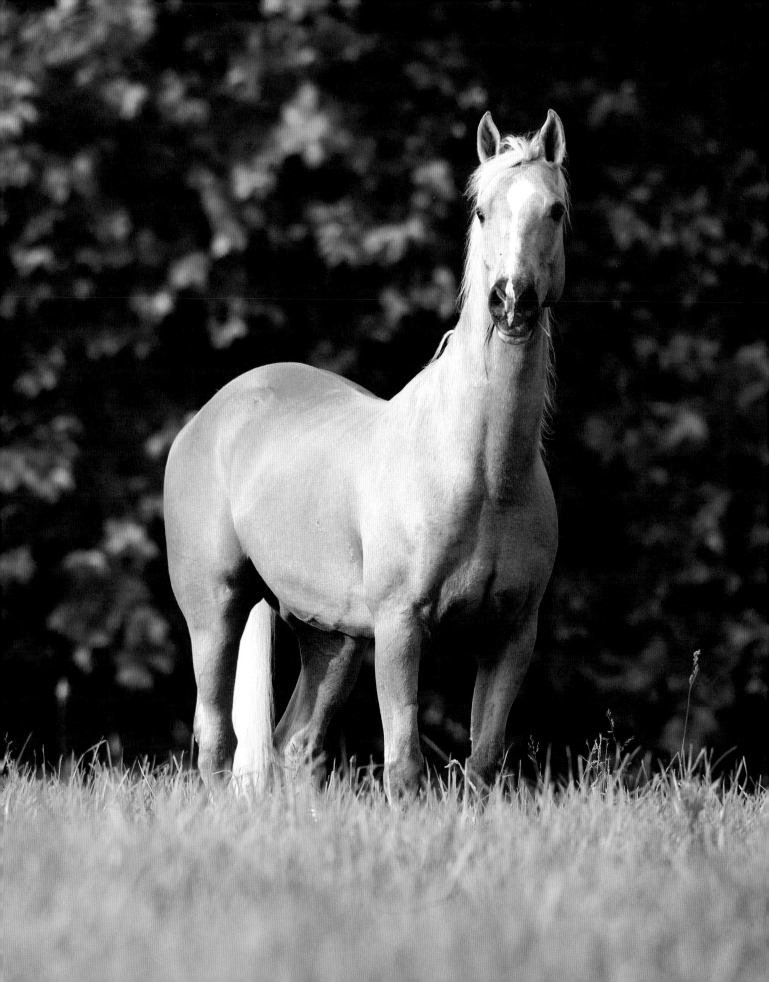

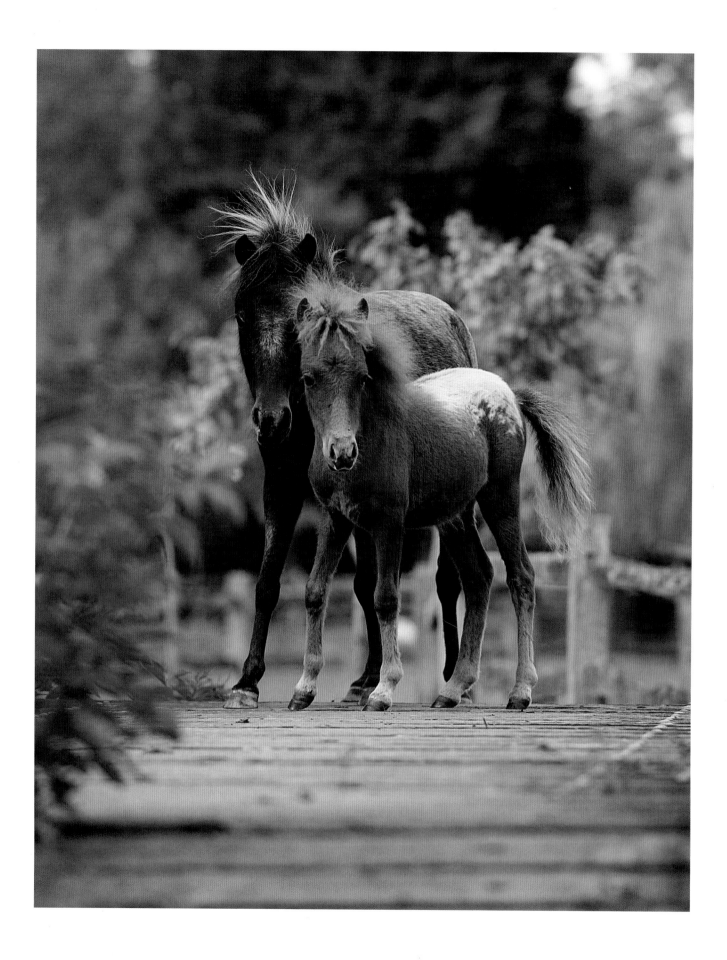

Falabella

Harsh conditions among the pampas of South America shaped the Falabella, the perfect horse in miniature. Said to be the original miniature horse, it has been bred on the Falabella ranch in Argentina for more than 150 years. It was almost certainly based on the Spanish stock brought to the New World, then abandoned to fend for itself when the would-be conquerors were forced to flee. In order to cope with the climate of the pampas – where cold winds, a blazing sun and furious storms are common – the horse had to adapt physiologically as well as mentally.

In 1845 an Irishman called Patrick Newtall discovered that Native American tribes living in the pampas kept some unusually small horses among their more normal-sized stock. He obtained some and, with selective breeding, by 1853 had created a herd of horses standing no more than 40 inches tall. In 1879 he transferred his findings and the herd to his son-in-law, Juan Falabella.

Using other breeds to refine and define these little horses, among them some small English Thoroughbreds, Shetland ponies and Criollos, the Falabella family continues to breed miniatures today, and they are in high demand. John F. Kennedy is known to have been among the first to buy some Falabellas when the breeders made them available to selected clients.

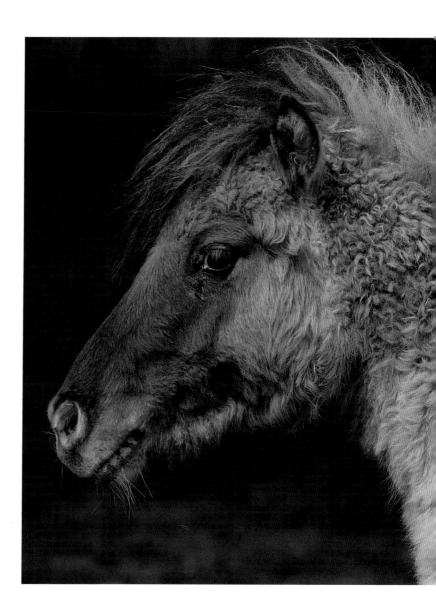

Opposite Despite its tiny stature – today 28–34 inches high, or the size of a dog – the Falabella is regarded as a horse in miniature.

Above The Falabella's head is neatly made and somewhat large in proportion to its body, with a relatively stout neck.

Paso Fino

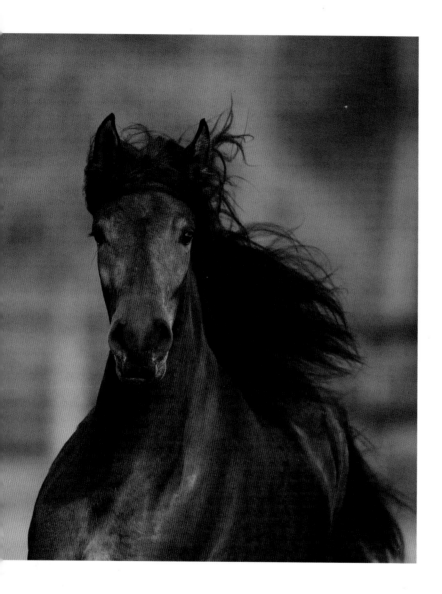

On his second voyage to the New World, Christopher Columbus brought the first horses into Santo Domingo – now the Dominican Republic. They were the Andalusian, Barb and Spanish Jennet (the latter an ancient breed that is now extinct, although efforts are being made to recreate it). The offspring of these first horses were dispersed to different countries during subsequent explorations and invasions, through Puerto Rico, Columbia, Panama, Mexico and Cuba, but the comparative isolation of their first home resulted in a recognizable fixed type.

Compact but muscular, with a refined head, gracefully arching neck and strong sound legs, Paso Fino horses inherited from the Jennet a comfortable smooth gait – the 'fine step', or *paso fino* – that was to give the breed its name. This four-beat lateral gait is the birthright of every Paso Fino – the first steps taken by newborn foals are in gait. The *paso fino* is rhythmic, with equal intervals between each hoof beat, and there is very little up and down movement, front or behind, which makes it easy on the rider. The gait may be performed at three speeds.

There are more than 200,000 Paso Fino horses throughout Central and South America, and the breed has proven its versatility in the showring, trail and endurance rides, dressage, rodeos and ranching.

Above The Paso Fino's noble good looks are indicative of its Spanish heritage. Most solid colours appear in the breed, with bay being relatively common.

Right A noble profile and bold eye are typical of the powerful and good-looking Paso Fino. The breed is both spirited and willing.

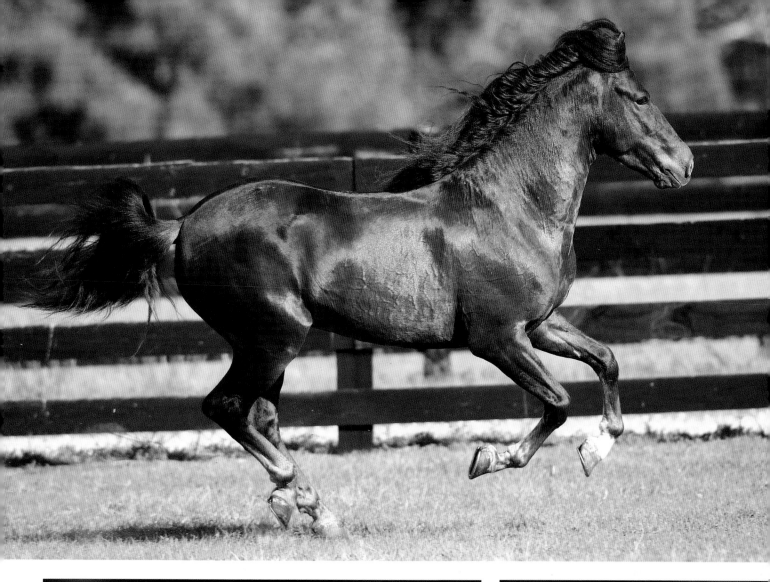

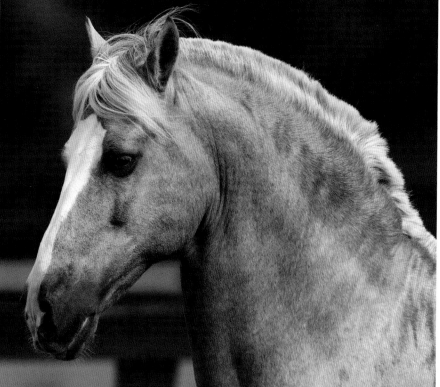

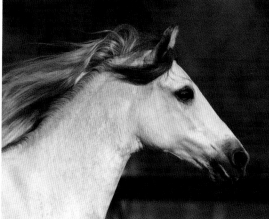

Top Although the Paso Fino stands at little over 14hh, it is a relatively powerful breed that is generally a suitable mount for adults.

Above The Paso Fino usually has a straight profile and carries its fine head high.

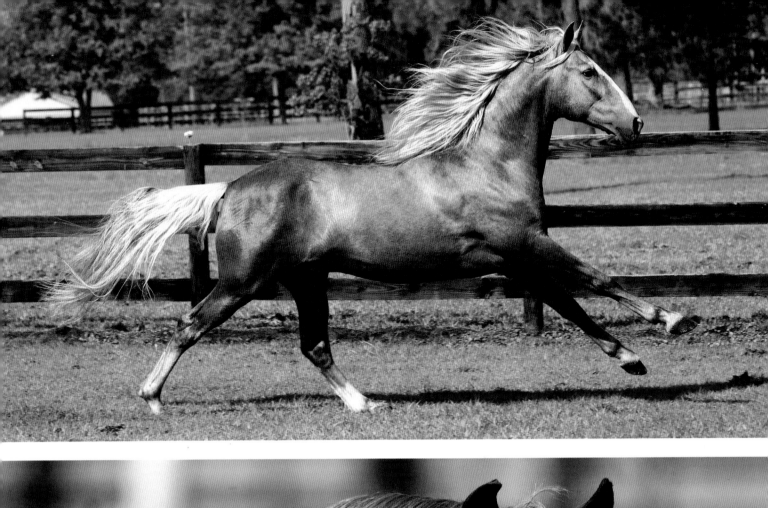
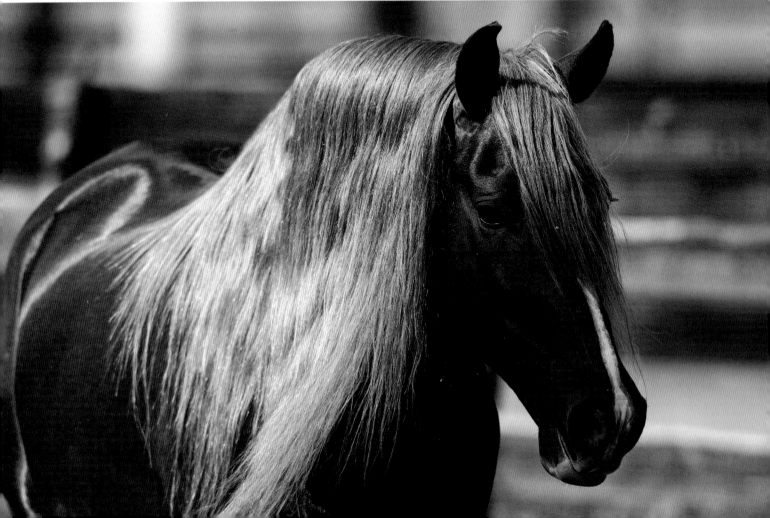

Peruvian Paso

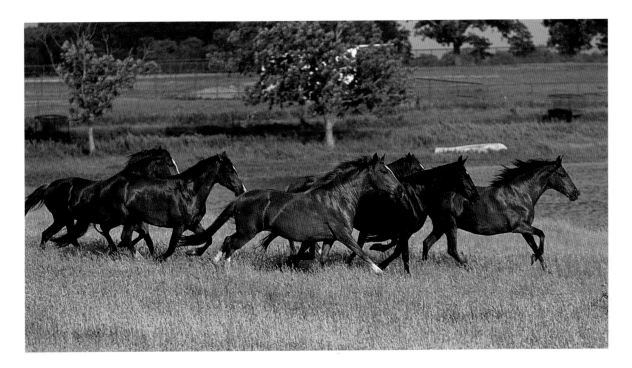

Although the Peruvian Paso and the Paso Fino share many attributes, they are two separate breeds. They are undoubtedly based on the same or similar Spanish ancestors, but the Peruvian, once established, was maintained in its native country as 'the national horse of Peru'. Its breeders have every right to be proud, for the Peruvian Paso is an athletic, handsome creature, with presence, stamina, excellent conformation and an exceptionally sweet temper. It was selectively bred using only horses that were good natured, so its temperament became as much a part of the breed as its appearance.

The Peruvian Paso is the epitome of energy, grace and refinement. Its natural gaits – inherited from the Spanish Jennet – include the smooth four-beat lateral gait. Uniquely, it also has the *termino*, a graceful, flowing action in which the horse rolls its forelegs to the outside as it strides forwards in a move much like a swimmer's arm motion. Like all its gaits, this is always passed on to its foals. The Peruvians maintain that their national horse has another unique attribute – that of *brio*. This is a quality of spirit that enables this glorious breed to perform with an arrogance and exuberance that is thrilling to watch.

Opposite top This superb Peruvian Paso demonstrates the attribute of *brio* – an indefinable quality of spirit.

Opposite below With its straight profile and crested neck, the Peruvian Paso is one of the most beautiful breeds.

Above These Peruvian Pasos display the breed's natural agility and balance.

Mangalarga Marchador

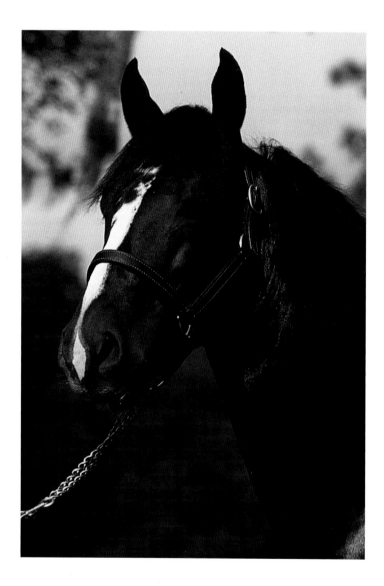

Brazil's national breed takes its melodious name from the Hacienda Mangalarga, where it was founded, and the *marcha*, its smooth, rhythmic gait. The *marcha picada* is a lateral gait, while the *marcha batida* is diagonal. The *batida* (meaning 'to hit') is less smooth than the *picada* (meaning 'light touch'), in which there is very little vertical movement and which is therefore more comfortable. The smooth gait was ideal for the farmers and ranchers of Brazil, who spent most of their days in the saddle.

The Portuguese royal family brought horses to Brazil in 1807, when it fled Napoleon's armies. A stallion aptly named Sublime, descended from these horses, was the founder of the Mangalarga Marchador. After being gifted to an established breeding farm called Hacienda Campo Alegre, in the state of Minas Gerais, Sublime was put to Spanish mares, the offspring of which were known as 'Sublime horses'. Some of these were acquired by the Hacienda Mangalarga.

The Mangalarga Marchador has been bred for 180 years with no other bloodlines used as outcrosses. Some Arab, Thoroughbred and American Saddlebred blood was introduced to breeding programmes in Sao Paolo, a neighbouring state to Minas Gerais, which led to a separate registry being set up for Mangalarga Paulista horses.

Above The Mangalarga Marchador's straight profile is reminiscent of the Barb's, perhaps as a result of its heritage.

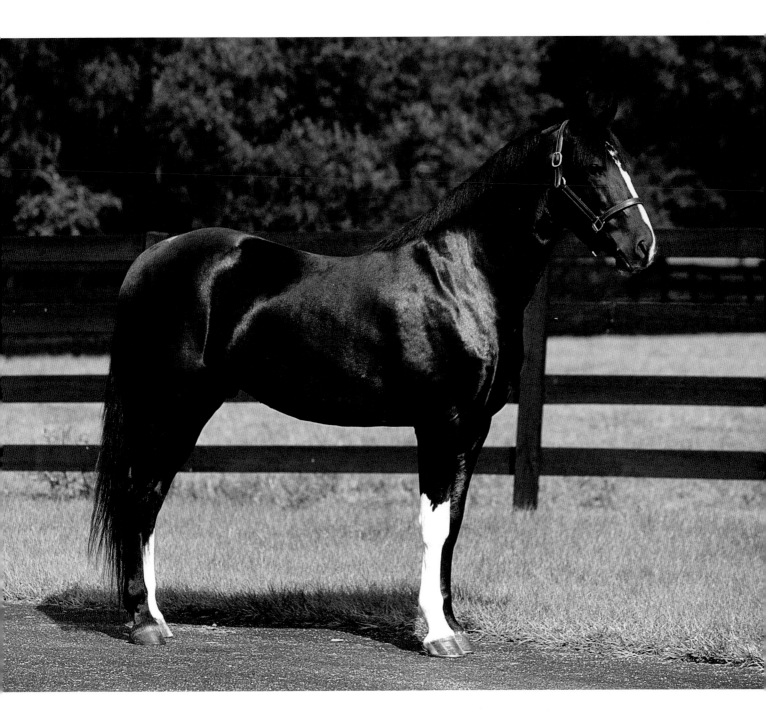

Above The Marchador has a quality head, elegant neck, medium-length back and powerful quarters.

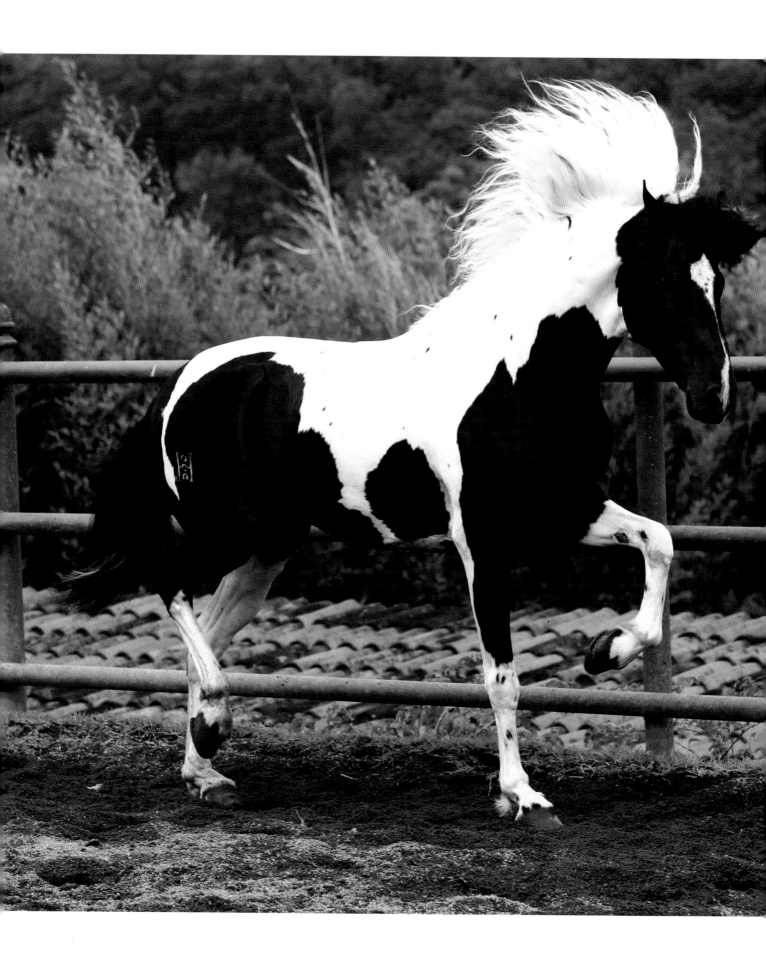

Criollo

Next to the Arab the Criollo is arguably the best endurance horse in the world, due to its early beginnings in one of the harshest environments on Earth. The Criollo breed traces back to a shipment of Spanish horses to the Rio de la Plata, the estuary formed by the confluence of the Paraná and Uruguay rivers, between Uruguay and Argentina. The horses were imported by Pedro de Mendoza, the founder of Buenos Aires. When the Spanish invaders were forced to abandon Buenos Aires in 1540, they released up to 45 horses; by 1580 the feral horse population was estimated at 12,000.

In 1925–8 an Argentine adventurer named A.F. Tschiffely rode from Beunos Aires, Argentina, to Washington DC – a distance of some 10,000 miles – on two Criollo horses, both of which lived into old age. Much later, a ranch owner named Jorge Saenz Rosas lent his Criollo, Sufridor, for a horseback ride from the Beagle Channel in Tierra del Fuego up to the shores of the Arctic Ocean in Deadhorse, Alaska. The ride was completed in five and a half years, ending in 1993 – it can be claimed that Sufridor has probably travelled the furthest distance of any horse in a single direction.

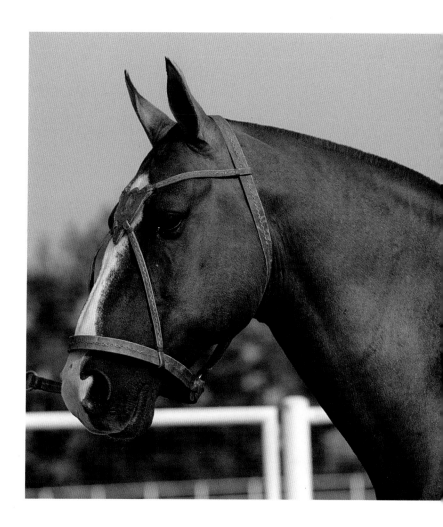

Opposite All coat colours can be seen in the Criollo, including piebald like in this one, as well as spotted.

Above The Criollo's straight or convex head and muscular neck are testimony to its Spanish ancestry.

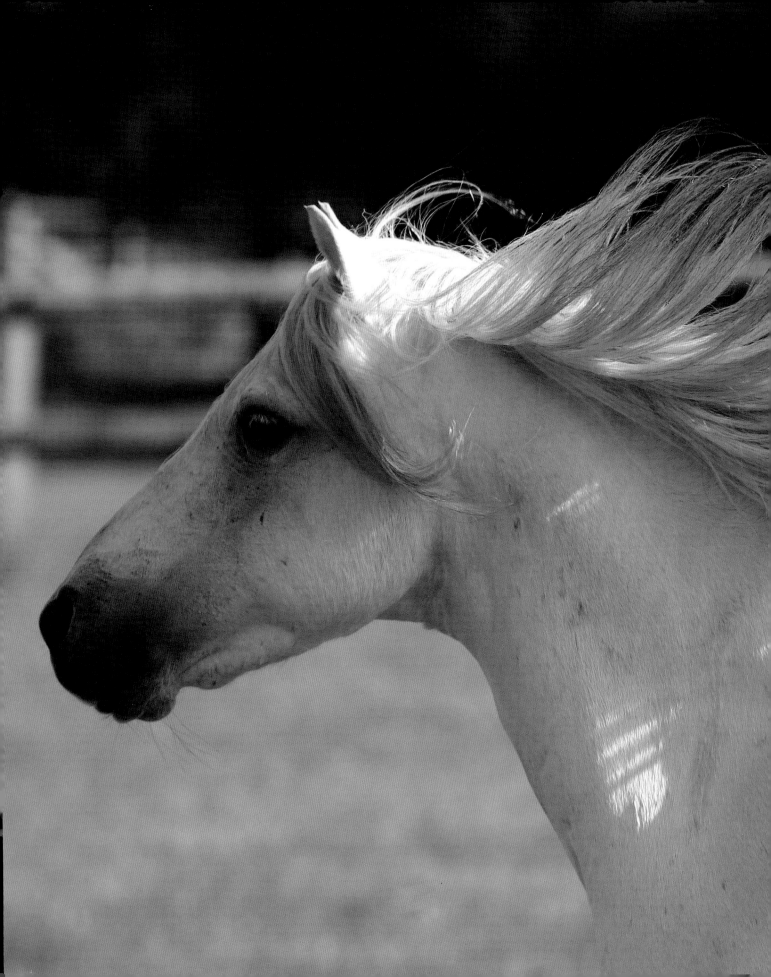

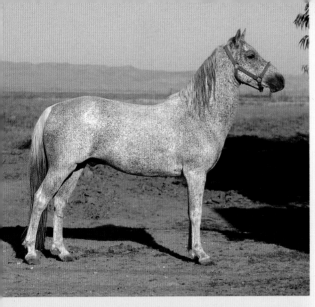

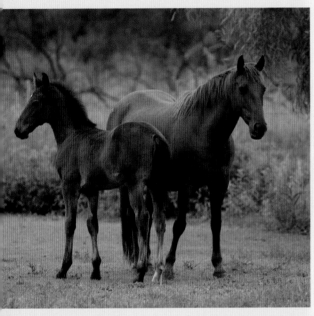

Rest of the World

The glorious Orlov Trotter was developed in Russia specifically for carriage driving, Indonesia's little ponies contributed to the mighty Boerperd of South Africa, and the Marwari of the Indian subcontinent, with its delightfully curled ears, displays its Arab heritage. The world's horse breeds are as diverse as they are enchanting.

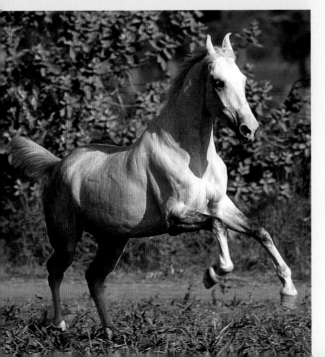

Clockwise from far left Caspian (page 146); Iomud (page 149); Australian Stock Horse (page 154); Marwari (page 150).

Caspian

A perfect horse in miniature, the Caspian is an ancient breed. It was thought to be extinct until 1965, when American horse enthusiast Louise Firouz saw a bay stallion on the southern shores of the Caspian Sea, in what used to be called Persia and is now Iran. It was like nothing she had read about or seen before: small and well proportioned, it appeared to be a scaled down version of an Arab horse.

Firouz was struck by the little horse's similarity to equines depicted on rock carvings at the ancient Persian capital of Persepolis. There is further evidence that the breed may have existed centuries ago – small horses of Caspian type are depicted on the ancient seal of Darius the Great, King of Persia (522–486BC).

Firouz estimated that there were only 50 Caspian horses along the whole southern coast of the Caspian Sea – about 30 of these occupying an area of 2,000 square miles between Amol, Babol and Kiakola in the Elburz Mountains. She acquired six stallions and seven mares, and founded a breeding herd. 'They are built to carry the weight of a child, with the gait of a horse and, except at full gallop, the speed of a horse', observed Firouz, whose efforts in breeding Caspians are widely credited with saving the breed.

Right The Caspian is like an Arab in miniature, with a short, fine head, large eyes, short ears, and a slim and graceful body.

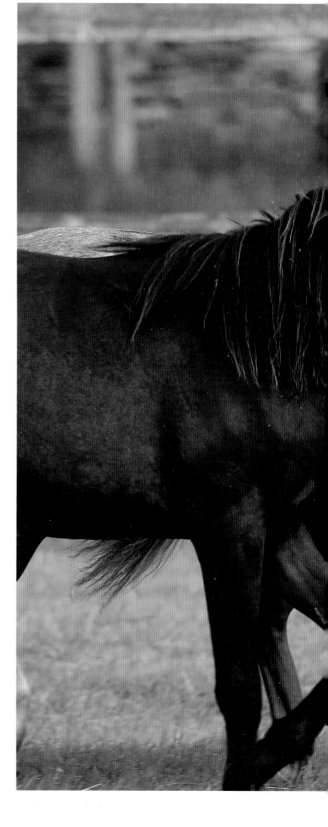

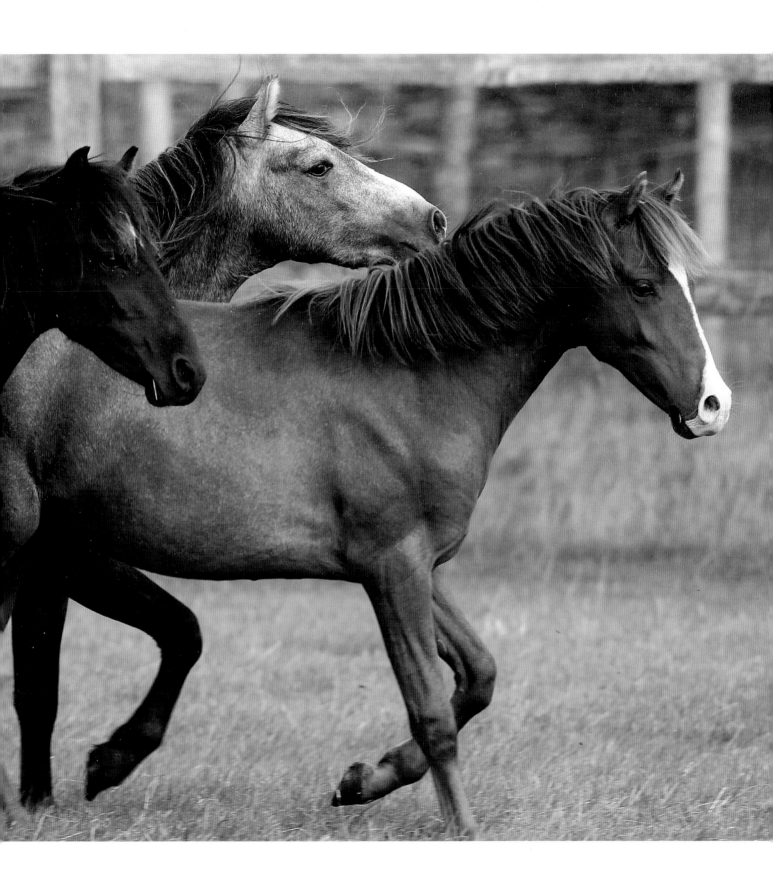

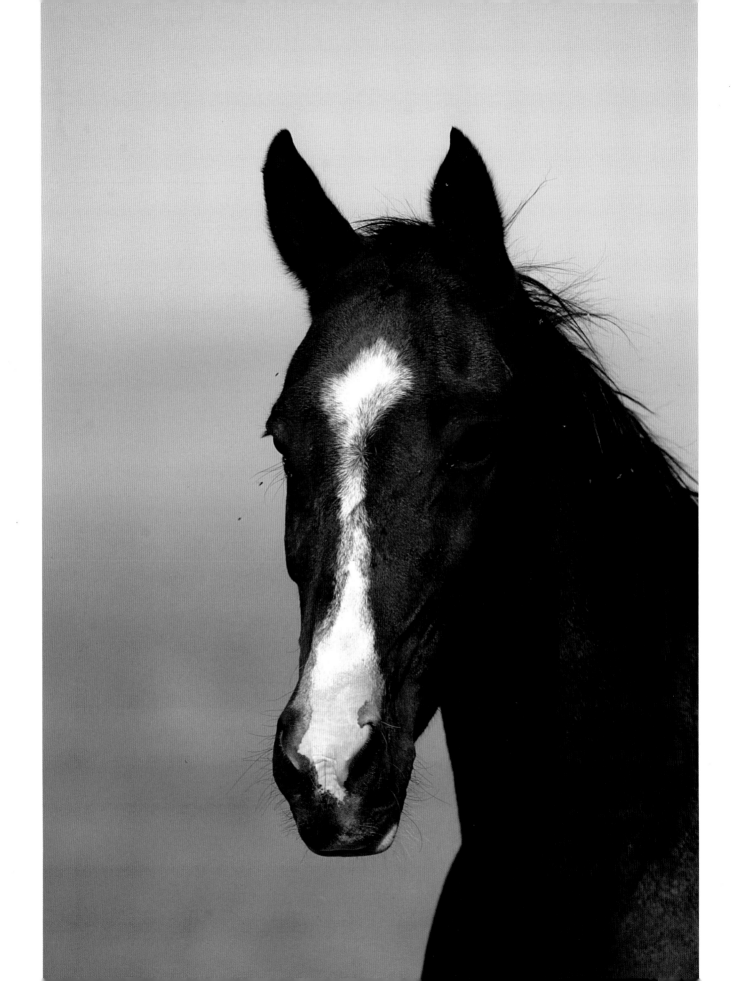

Iomud

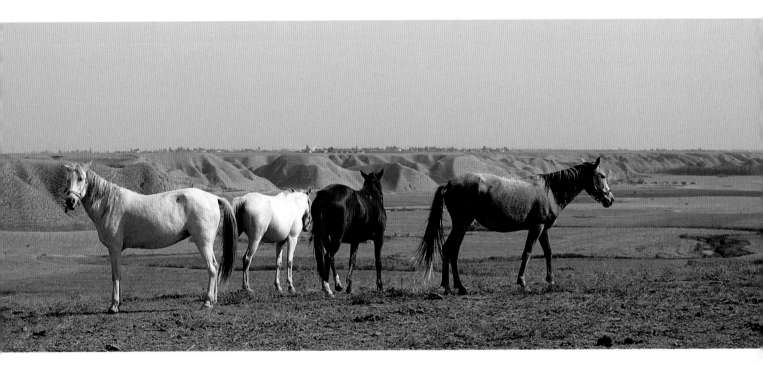

The Iomud – also known as the Yomud or Yamud – is to be found in northern Iran and Turkmenistan, and is thought to be more closely related to the Akhal-Teke than to the Caspian. It was developed by the Iomud tribe, who inhabited the Tashauz oasis in the arid desert of southern Turkmenistan. It is undoubtedly based on the old Turkmen horses and has, over the centuries, been influenced by Mongolian blood as well as infusions of Arab blood during the 14th century. It is also likely that Kazakh horses have played a role in its development.

The Iomud was kept in herds. Like the Akhal-Teke it developed a supreme toughness, with the ability to withstand extremes of temperature and eke out an existence on minimal rations. While it lacks the speed and beauty of the Akhal-Teke, it has every bit of its endurance and stamina. It also possesses a natural jumping ability and is long lived.

In the late 20th century the Iomud was in very real danger of extinction, with just 616 pure-breds remaining in 1989. Studs were established in the 1980s to increase the numbers, and a conservation farm was set up in Kyzyl-Atrek in Turkmenistan.

Opposite There is undoubtedly Oriental blood in the Iomud, although the breed lacks the exceptional beauty of the Arab.

Above The Iomud is lean and wiry, typical of a desert breed, and well adapted to the harsh environment in which it lives.

Marwari

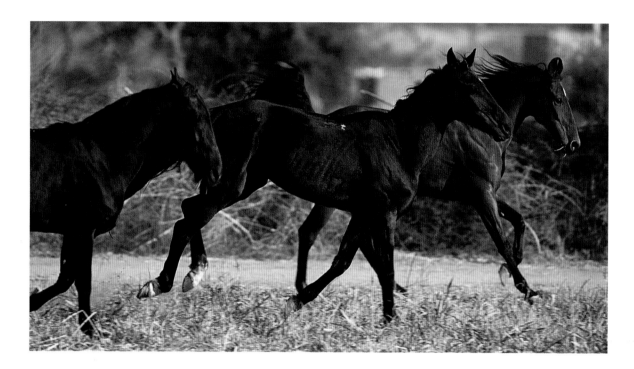

In its native India the Marwari was once considered divine and superior to all men, including those of royal blood. Only the Rajput families and the Kshatriyas warrior caste were permitted to ride these exalted equines in feudal times.

A Rajput warrior clan, the Rathores, was forced from the kingdom of Kannauj in the 1100s and resettled in an area called Maru Pradesh, or 'the land of death'. The warring clan's resilient Marwari horses were very capable of surviving in this unforgiving region and serving as cavalry mounts. Renowned for its homing instinct, the Marwari has an unerring ability to bring back riders who get lost in the desert, and its exceptional hearing provides an early warning of impending danger. It was said that there were only three ways a Marwari would leave a battlefield: if he was victorious, if he was carrying his wounded master to safety or when he was eaten by vultures after laying down his life for his master.

In the 20th century there was no longer a need for a battle horse and the numbers of Marwaris dropped sharply. The ruling caste of Marwar – also known as Jodhpur – has, however, played an active role in saving and promoting India's national breed.

Above The elegant Marwari can be found in all coat colours, with grey – considered auspicious – being the most popular.

Opposite The distinctive curled ears of the Marwari are only otherwise seen in the Kathiawari, to which it is closely related.

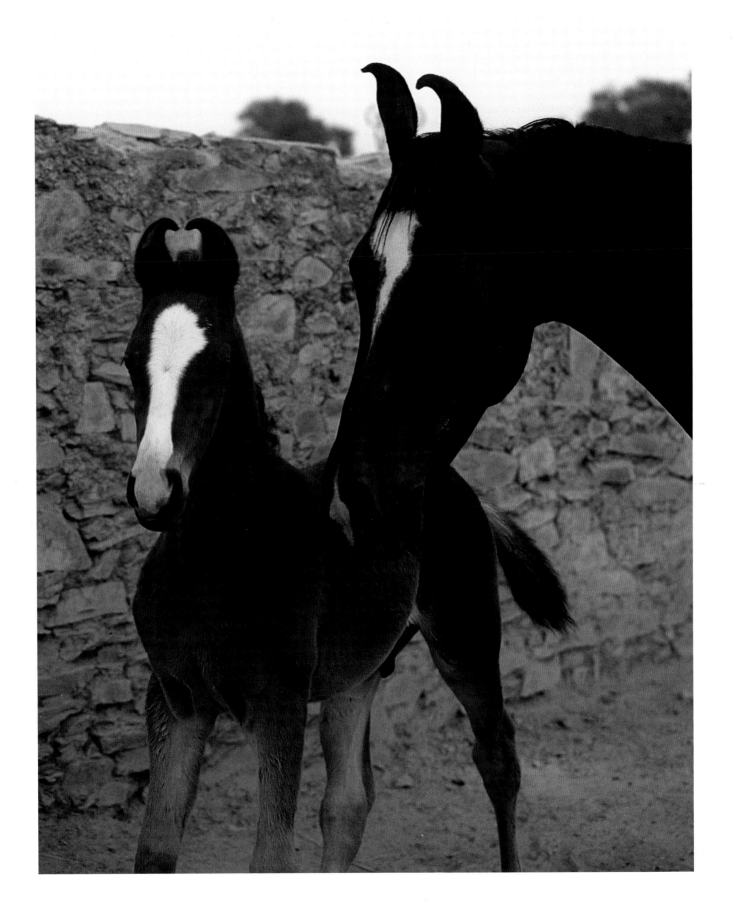

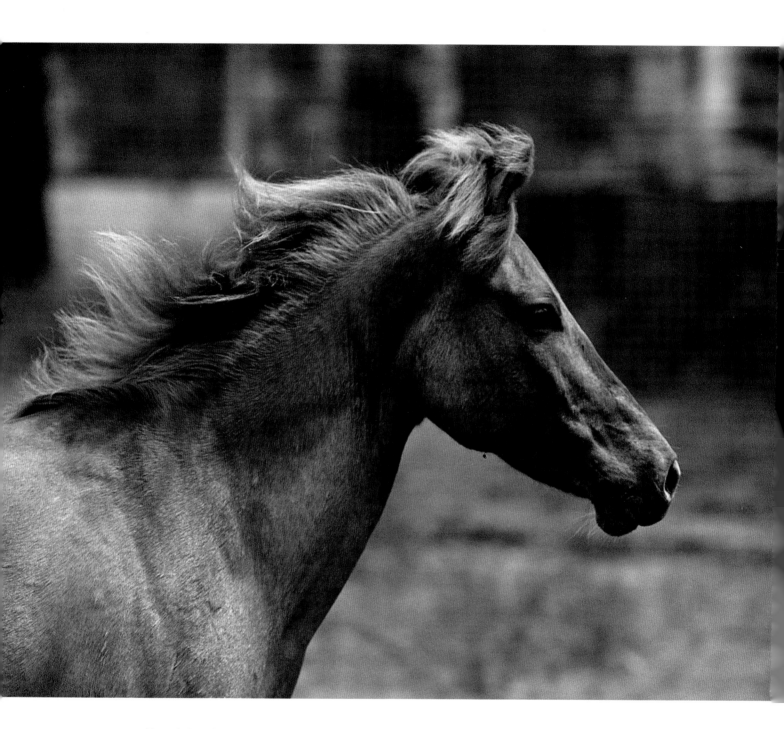

Above Indonesia's equine breeds are all
similar, the Batak being selectively bred
in Sumatra.

Indonesian Breeds

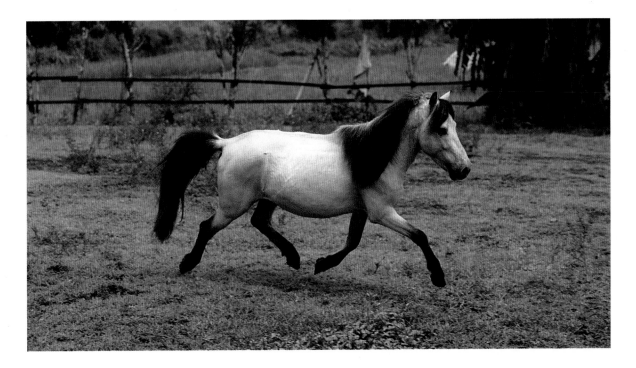

Indonesia's tropical islands are home to a total of eight equine breeds; they are all similar, with Mongolian and Arab influences. The Dutch East India Company played a part in the development of the Indonesian breeds through its introduction of Oriental horses to the islands. Its first factory was established on the island of Java during the 16th century, and from that time on the company imported harness horses and packhorses.

A large part of the ponies' heritage is due to the crossing of local stock with imported Arab and Barb horses. The finest breed is the Sandalwood, which comes from the islands of Sumba and Sumbawa (it is often referred to as the Sumba-Sumbawa pony). It takes its official name from the sandalwood trees that grow prolifically on the islands. The Batak originates in Sumatra, the largest Indonesian island, where it is selectively bred. It is highly regarded by the Indonesian people and is also used to improve the country's other breeds, including the Sandalwood, Java and Timor. The Timor is the smallest of the Indonesian ponies, standing at little more than 12hh. All the breeds are wiry and tough and make good riding ponies, as well as pulling the *sados* (carts).

Above The Sandalwood pony is used as a packhorse, for riding and for light draft work; it usually stands at around 13hh.

Australian Stock Horse

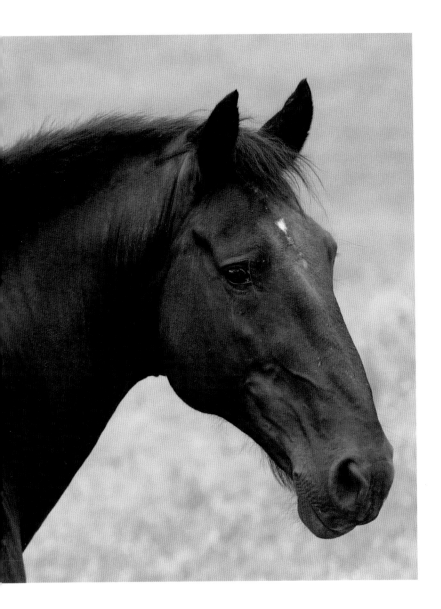

Sometimes also called the Waler, the Australian Stock Horse is a strong utilitarian breed that is descended from the horses sent from Britain to Australia by the First Fleet in 1788, to establish the first European colony. The horses were a mix of Arab, Thoroughbred and Spanish stock, and those that survived the long voyage of 9–12 months were the toughest individuals.

More challenges awaited the horses in the strange and uncharted land, and as the settlers ventured inland their robust horses became invaluable. Explorers, stockmen, bushrangers and troopers relied on them utterly. Further infusions of Arab, Thoroughbred and Indonesian Timor pony blood from Indonesia, as well as that of Welsh stock from Britain, resulted in a handsome, resilient equine. The horses were named Walers after the colony of New South Wales – the first to be settled – although they spread all over the vast new continent.

As well as being an excellent stock horse the breed made a superb cavalry mount – in 1857, 29 Walers were sent from Sydney to Calcutta as British Army mounts, with a further 2,500 exported a year later. During the Boer War, Australia's national horse was exported in even greater numbers. In 1899–1902 around 16,000 Walers were serving in several regiments, including the Lancers, Commonwealth Horse, Mounted Rifles and Bushmen's Troop.

Above The Australian Stock Horse is based on Thoroughbred and Spanish bloodlines, which are obvious in its profile.

Opposite top All colours can be found in the Australian Stock Horse, although it is predominantly bay.

Opposite below The breed stands at around 16.2hh and is well put together, making it suitable for competition as well as riding.

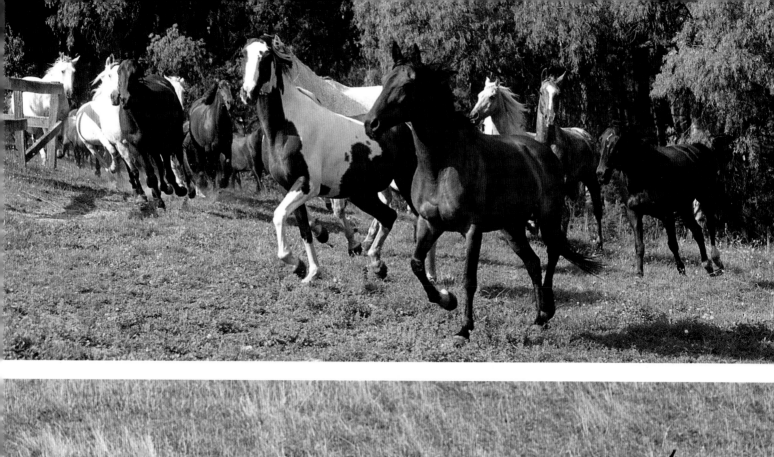

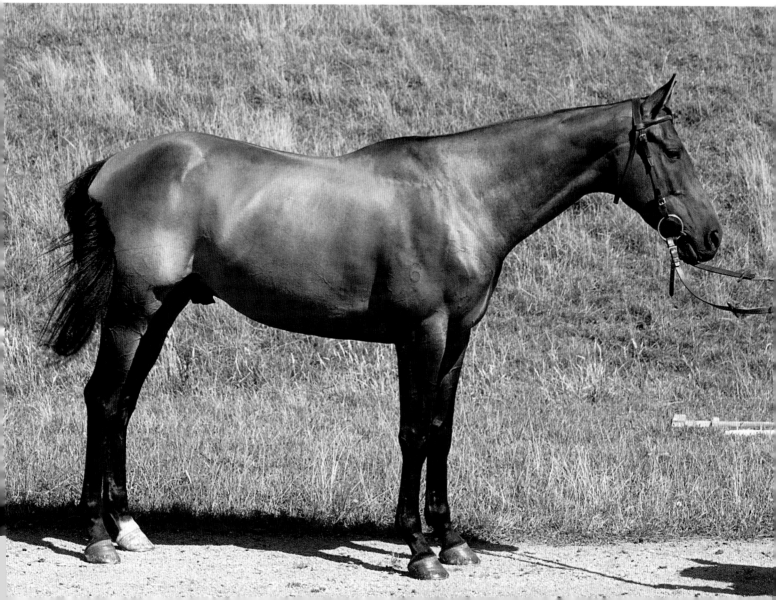

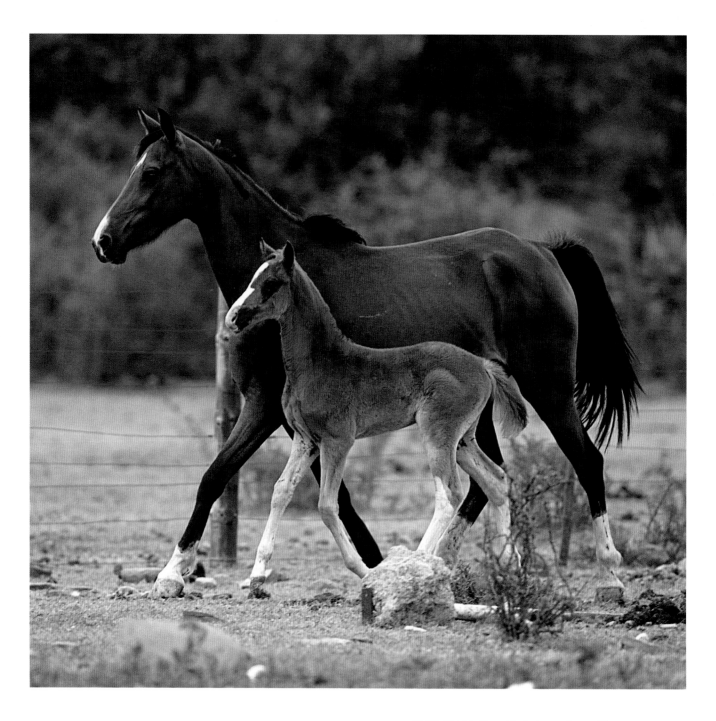

Above The handsome foal shown above will
grow to around 15hh and already has the
slender but well-formed legs of its breed.

Boerperd

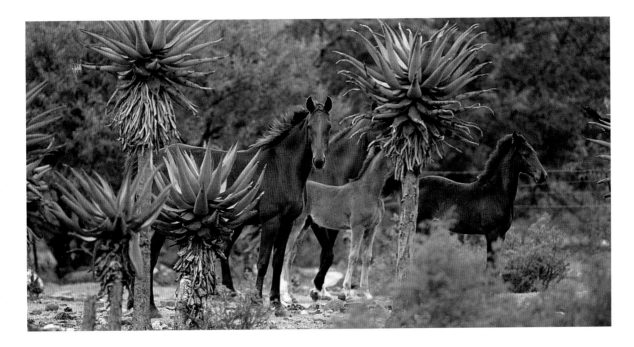

When Dutch white settlers took advantage of the sea passage that established a route between the Cape of Good Hope and south Asia (discovered by a Portuguese sailor in the 17th century), they introduced small horses from the island of Java to South Africa. These equines were gaited – that is they had a fifth, lateral gait – and were able to cope with the heat on the vast African continent. Arab, Barb and Iberian bloodlines were introduced for size and quality.

It is fair to say that the growth and development of the Boerperd horse, or Boer, are inseparable from the history of the white settlers. When the Boers

(a Dutch/Afrikaans term for farmers) spread east and north-east across Africa from the Cape of Good Hope in a migration known as the Great Trek, their horses went with them.

The durable Boerperd was in great demand as a cavalry horse due to its surefootedness, stamina and intelligence, as well as its comfortable gait. It was later improved with infusions of Thoroughbred blood, as well as (probably) some Quarter Horse. Thousands of horses were shipped to South Africa from America to mount soldiers in the Boer Wars, among them some 20,000 Quarter Horses from a breeder in Galveston, Texas.

Above Boerperd mares and foals in their native South Africa. The horses occur in a variety of colours, including black, brown, bay, chestnut, grey, dun, roan and palomino.

Orlov Trotter

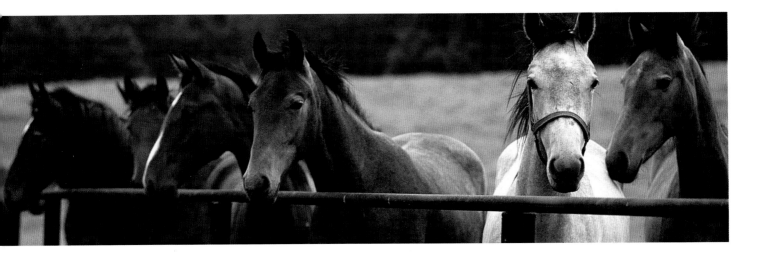

When Count Alexei Orlov was gifted land by Catherine the Great, Empress of Russia, for his part in the late 18th-century coup that brought her to the throne, he founded a stud farm at Khrenovsky, in central Russia, to breed the strong and elegant, fast-trotting horses that were to bear his name. His aim was to produce handsome equines that could cope with Russia's climate and have the ability to traverse her vast spaces with ease.

Count Orlov purchased a pure-bred grey Arab stallion called Smetanka in Turkey for the then staggering sum of 60,000 roubles. Long backed for an Arab – an autopsy found that he possessed an extra rib – Smetanka produced a colt called Polkan, the offspring out of a mare purchased by Count Orlov from the Frederiksborg Royal Stud. Orlov continued to breed European-type mares to Polkan;

these included Friesians, since the old Dutch breed was renowned for its trot. Among the offspring was a grey colt named Bars I. Generally considered to be the founding sire of the Orlov Trotter, Bars was foaled in 1784. An imposing horse, despite his size he possessed admirable agility and a swift, elegant trot. He produced, among others, two sons – the black Liubeznyi I and the grey Lebed' I – to whom all modern Orlov Trotters trace back.

With its ground-covering stride, the Orlov Trotter was the most popular breed for pulling the troika. Initially developed to carry the mail swiftly in difficult, snowy terrain, troikas are harnessed with three horses abreast. The centre horse moves at an extended trot, while the other two move at a canter, with the three-horse arrangement being much more stable than the two-horse carriage used in Europe.

Above Due to its Arab heritage the Orlov Trotter is often grey; other colours include black, bay and chestnut.

Opposite top The Orlov Trotter is a popular choice for pulling the troika in a unique three-abreast formation.

Opposite below One of the most elegant of equines, the Orlov Trotter stands at an imposing 17hh.

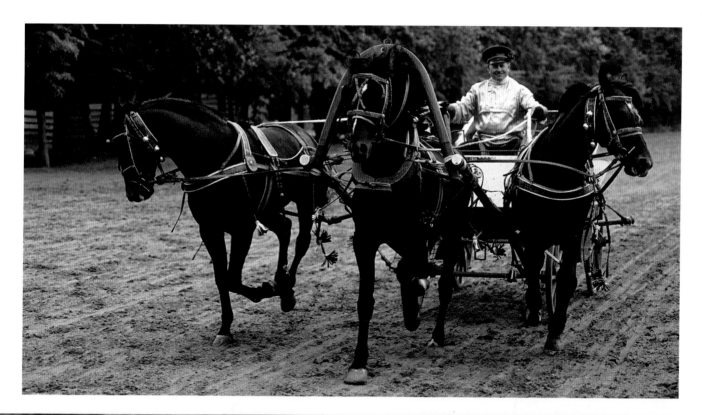

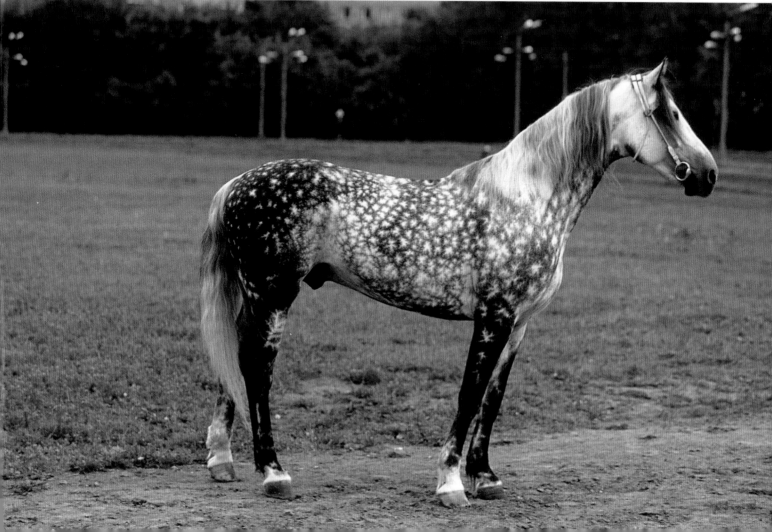

Index